A Hotel Manager's
HANDBOOK

A Hotel Manager's HANDBOOK

189 Techniques for Achieving Exceptional Guest Satisfaction

Vincent P. Magnini, PhD
and
Carol J. Simon, MBA

APPLE
ACADEMIC
PRESS

Apple Academic Press Inc. | Apple Academic Press Inc.
3333 Mistwell Crescent | 9 Spinnaker Way
Oakville, ON L6L 0A2 | Waretown, NJ 08758
Canada | USA

©2016 by Apple Academic Press, Inc.

Exclusive worldwide distribution by CRC Press, a member of Taylor & Francis Group

No claim to original U.S. Government works

Printed in the United States of America on acid-free paper

International Standard Book Number-13: 978-1-77188-348-1 (Paperback)

International Standard Book Number-13: 978-1-77188-349-8 (eBook)

Typeset by Accent Premedia Services (www.accentpremedia.com)

Library and Archives Canada Cataloguing in Publication

Magnini, Vincent P., author
A hotel manager's handbook : 189 techniques for achieving exceptional guest satisfaction / Vincent P. Magnini, PhD & Carol J. Simon, MBA.

Includes bibliographical references and index.
Issued in print and electronic formats.
ISBN 978-1-77188-348-1 (paperback).--ISBN 978-1-77188-349-8 (pdf)
1. Hotel management--Handbooks, manuals, etc. I. Simon, Carol J., author II. Title.

TX911.3.M27M3345 2015   647.94068   C2015-906686-7   C2015-906687-5

Library of Congress Cataloging-in-Publication Data

Names: Simon, Carol J., 1956- author. | Simon, Carol J., author.
Title: A hotel manager's handbook : 189 techniques for achieving exceptional guest satisfaction / Vincent P. Magnini, PhD & Carol J. Simon, MBA.
Description: Toronto ; Waretown, N.J. : Apple Academic Press, 2015. |

Includes bibliographical references and index.
Identifiers: LCCN 2015037177 | ISBN 9781771883481 (alk. paper)
Subjects: LCSH: Hotel management--Handbooks, manuals, etc.
Classification: LCC TX911.3.M27 S55 2015 | DDC 647.94068--dc23
LC record available at http://lccn.loc.gov/2015037177

Apple Academic Press also publishes its books in a variety of electronic formats. Some content that appears in print may not be available in electronic format. For information about Apple Academic Press products, visit our website at **www.appleacademicpress.com** and the CRC Press website at **www.crc-press.com**

Contents

About the Authors

. . . .

Vincent Magnini holds a PhD in International Business/Marketing from Old Dominion University, an MBA from Wichita State University, and a Bachelor's of Science in Hospitality and Tourism Management from Virginia Tech. He was recently ranked as one of the top 12 most prolific hospitality researchers worldwide. He has published five books and more than 100 articles and reports. Vince has been featured three times on National Public Radio's (NPR) "With Good Reason", once on NPR's "All Things Considered" and cited in the *New York Times*.

Carol Simon holds an MBA from Golden Gate University and a Bachelor's of Science in Business from Arizona State University. She has over 35 years of hotel experience including resorts, full-service hotels, select-service hotels, as well as a regional role. In addition, Carol has taught college-level hospitality classes and has served on various tourism and community service boards. She has received the Georgia Hotelier of the Year Award as well as awards for achieving outstanding guest service and financial success from her hotels.

Responsible Practice

• • • • • • • • • • • • • • • •

The techniques contained in this book should be used responsibly at hotels and only used when deemed appropriate by management. The authors and/or publishing company cannot be held responsible for any potentially negative outcomes.

Introduction

● ● ● ● ● ● ● ● ● ● ● ● ● ● ● ● ●

As we all know, guest satisfaction is the lifeblood of any hotel. Short-term profitability may not depend on guest satisfaction, but long-run hotel profitability and prosperity most certainly does. The positive word-of-mouth has long been a key determinant of success in the hotel business, and it carries even more influence today due to the proliferation of travel blogs. Word-of-mouth (both positive and negative) travels faster and carries more weight in today's hotel business than ever before. Thus, it is more important than ever before to leave guests highly satisfied.

A number of useful books have been written about hotel guest satisfaction, but this book differs from others in two important ways. First, many of the existing books require the reader to sift through pages of narratives in order to identify actionable tactics and strategies that can be applied at the property-level. In contrast, the current book articulates one unique and actionable customer satisfaction technique on each page. Therefore, groups of managers within a property can read and discuss a given technique and collectively decide if it is appropriate for implementation at their given property.

The second way in which this book brings value to hoteliers is through the backgrounds of the two authors. Author Vince Magnini spent about 10 years in the hotel business at both branded and independent properties, but then left hotel management to earn a PhD in marketing. Since being awarded his doctorate, he has been an active researcher and was recently ranked as one of the top 12 most prolific hospitality researchers in the world. Therefore, the customer satisfaction techniques written by Vince in this book are grounded with knowledge of the latest research in our industry.

The other author, Carol Simon, brings a different perspective. Carol spent more than 30 years in hotel management prior to her retirement in 2014 and is now doing consulting. She was an award-winning general manager as well as an area manager overseeing multiple hotel properties. Consequently, Carol contributes techniques to the book that are both creative and practical. It is prudent to note, however, that Carol's knowledge is also well-grounded and informed because she holds an MBA and has taught at the University level for a number of years.

For hotel management readers: If you are currently on a hotel management team and reading this book, it is hoped that you will find enough of the 189 techniques in this book, which are useful and applicable to feel as if this book has been a wise investment of your time and money. Each page that offers a technique (all 189) allows the reader an opportunity to denote whether the technique should be applied in the reader's property and also prompts the reader to assign a responsible party and implementation date.

For hospitality student readers: If you are a student preparing for a career in hotel management, this book will provide you with an arsenal of creative tools as you begin your career. Because many of the techniques presented in this book were located by the authors at hotels outside of the U.S., being aware of them should allow new entrants in hotel management to be on the leading edge of customer service innovation.

The customer service techniques in this book cover each stage of the guest experience, but also extend further to address areas needed to cultivate a culture of service excellence. The performance of hotel associates is a function of both their abilities and motivation levels; therefore, techniques related to areas of employee recruitment, selection, training, and evaluation are key components in this book. It is hoped that all readers (managers and future managers) will find this book motivating and energizing.

1	2	3	4	5	6	7	8	9	10
11	12	13	14	15	16	17	18	19	20
21	22	23	24	25	26	27	28	29	30
31	32	33	34	35	36	37	38	39	40
41	42	43	44	45	46	47	48	49	50
51	52	53	54	55	56	57	58	59	60
61	62	63	64	65	66	67	68	69	70
71	72	73	74	75	76	77	78	79	80
81	82	83	84	85	86	87	88	89	90
91	92	93	94	95	96	97	98	99	100
101	102	103	104	105	106	107	108	109	110
111	112	113	114	115	116	117	118	119	120
121	122	123	124	125	126	127	128	129	130
131	132	133	134	135	136	137	138	139	140
141	142	143	144	145	146	147	148	149	150
151	152	153	154	155	156	157	158	159	160
161	162	163	164	165	166	167	168	169	170
171	172	173	174	175	176	177	178	179	180
181	182	183	184	185	186	187	188	189	

Section I

● ● ● ● ● ● ● ● ● ● ● ● ● ● ● ●

Enabling the Service Experience

PREVIEW

The hotel business is inherently a people business; there is a very large human component in the industry. Guest satisfaction hinges upon the attitudes and actions of hotel associates. It seems appropriate, therefore, to dedicate the first section of this book to techniques aimed at maximizing the performance of line-level associates. Some techniques address pre-hiring activities involving recruitment and selection, some discuss training, and other techniques offer suggestions for improving the evaluation of team members.

Frontline Employee Recruitment and Selection

As we all know, guest-associate interactions have a heavy influence on the hospitality experience. Top-rate guest satisfaction scores rely upon hiring high-quality associates. Training and development during employment are evidently important as well, but much can be said about hiring the right person in the first place.

Come work here, we'll hire anyone.

This chapter, therefore, begins by presenting techniques that can be used to generate the best possible applicant pools for open positions. Position description announcements must be well-crafted and should convey not just the details regarding the open position, but also a sense of the company's personality and culture. High-quality prospects should be given the motivation to want to apply and become a part of the team. Strategies for getting the open position information out to the best-qualified prospective employees are unique to a hotel property's particular market; nevertheless, such strategies should be actively developed.

After recruitment techniques, this chapter then focuses attention on selection tactics that can be used to identify and retain the best candidate from within the applicant pool. Benefits can be found in 360-degree interviewing, panel interviewing, and multiple day interviewing. Strong behavioral questions are the backbone of an effective interview; examples of such are provided in this chapter.

Because creative associates can often serve guests better than dull and unimaginative ones, behavioral interviewing questions can be augmented with creativity assessments such as the divergence testing described in this chapter. Because associates who can solve problems have the potential to improve operational efficiency, critical thinking tasks can also be incorporated into the selection process.

Incorporating well-thought-out behavioral interviewing questions that are asked in 360-degree formats, panel-style formats, and in multiple day formats helps avoid the 'We'll hire anyone' message that some hospitality firms unknowingly communicate. Selection tactics such as creativity assessments and critical thinking tasks also help avoid the 'we'll hire anyone' message. In other words, highly refined and well-orchestrated selection processes make the applicants want to work at your hotel, because such well-managed processes signal to the applicant that the firm is well-managed in other facets of business operations as well.

If a candidate is performing nicely in the selection and interviewing stages, subtle techniques can be used to sell the firm to the candidate to increase the likelihood that s/he will accept an offer. Such techniques are also offered in this chapter.

 *Technique #1*

Design Creative Job Announcements

In order to draw a strong applicant pool for open positions, the position announcements must be well-crafted. The hotel's marketing department should either write or help edit such descriptions. Without sacrificing truth in advertising, creative-minded marketers can often produce more interesting and appealing announcements than those who are more operations-minded.

☐ We already practice this technique

☐ This technique would not be suitable for our operation

☐ We practiced this in the past and need to jumpstart

☐ We should implement this technique

Assigned to: _____

Projected Date of Implementation: _____

Technique #2

Foster Relationships with Educational Institutions

Often, the best line-level associates and entry-level managers can be drawn from trade schools, colleges, and universities that offer hospitality management programs. All hotels (even free-standing, independent hotels) should have active relationships with one or more hospitality educational institutions.

☐ We already practice this technique

☐ This technique would not be suitable for our operation

☐ We practiced this in the past and need to jumpstart

☐ We should implement this technique

Assigned to: _____

Projected Date of Implementation: _____

Technique #3

Participate in Career Events

A representative from the hotel's management team should speak at local high school career days. Not only does this exposure foster positive community relations, but also the students are a good source of potential employees for certain positions.

☐ We already practice this technique

☐ This technique would not be suitable for our operation

☐ We practiced this in the past and need to jumpstart

☐ We should implement this technique

Assigned to: _____

Projected Date of Implementation: _____

Technique #4

Encourage Employee Referrals

Line-level associates should be encouraged to recruit their friends for open positions. Because the line-level employee is knowledgeable about the hotel's working culture and also knows his/her friends, this combination of knowledge puts him/her in an informed position to assess the potential match.

☐　We already practice this technique

☐　This technique would not be suitable for our operation

☐　We practiced this in the past and need to jumpstart

☐　We should implement this technique

Assigned to: _____

Projected Date of Implementation: _____

 *Technique #5*

Utilize 360-Degree Interviewing

Utilize 360-degree interviewing in which a candidate is interviewed not only by who s/he will be reporting to, but also by peers and potential subordinates. While this approach mandates interview training, there are several benefits. Namely, when a candidate is interviewed by future subordinates, his/her emotional intelligence, and rapport-building skills can be assessed. The 360-degree interviewing also gives those involved a sense of buy-in and engenders an empowerment culture.

☐ We already practice this technique

☐ This technique would not be suitable for our operation

☐ We practiced this in the past and need to jumpstart

☐ We should implement this technique

Assigned to: _____

Projected Date of Implementation: _____

Technique #6

Use Panel-Style Interviewing

Front-of-the-house position candidates should be subjected to the panel-style interviewing in which they are interviewed by more than one person at once. Panel-style interviewing allows for the ability to test a candidate's confidence and conversational ability in a situation in which some would find intimidating. For the purpose of practicality, a panel interviewing approach can be combined with the 360 degree interviewing described in the previous technique.

☐ We already practice this technique

☐ This technique would not be suitable for our operation

☐ We practiced this in the past and need to jumpstart

☐ We should implement this technique

Assigned to: _____

Projected Date of Implementation: _____

Technique #7

Encourage Multiple-Day Interviewing

. . . .

Whenever possible, applicants for the line-level positions should be asked to return for interviews on more than one day in order to gauge their dependability and demeanor at various points in time.

- [ ] We already practice this technique
- [ ] This technique would not be suitable for our operation
- [ ] We practiced this in the past and need to jumpstart
- [ ] We should implement this technique

Assigned to: _____

Projected Date of Implementation: _____

Technique #8

Assess Applicant Conversational Ability

During interviews, front-of-the-house applicants should be asked questions that test their conversational abilities. One such question might include 'If an alien lands on earth, how would you describe to the alien how to make a peanut butter and jelly sandwich?'

☐ We already practice this technique

☐ This technique would not be suitable for our operation

☐ We practiced this in the past and need to jumpstart

☐ We should implement this technique

Assigned to: _____

Projected Date of Implementation: _____

Technique #9

Assess Applicant Creativity

During interviews, front-of-the-house applicants should be asked to complete tasks that assess their creative talents. For instance, they could be given four minutes to write all of the uses that can be thought of for an object (e.g., a blanket) and then given four more minutes to write all of the uses that can be thought of for a different object (e.g., a brick). This task is termed a divergence test, and responses can be rated based upon the following criteria [1]:

- Fluency—how many meaningful ideas are generated in response to the stimuli?

- Originality—how rare are the given responses?

- Elaboration—how much detail is contained in the responses?

☐ We already practice this technique

☐ This technique would not be suitable for our operation

☐ We practiced this in the past and need to jumpstart

☐ We should implement this technique

Assigned to: _____

Projected Date of Implementation: _____

Technique #10

Assess Applicant Team-Mentality

During interviews, front-of-the-house applicants should be asked to tell a story about a time when they delivered exceptional customer service experience either at a hotel or any other service business. Candidates who recount stories in which they worked with past coworkers to deliver the experience are likely more team-oriented than those who only discuss their own actions [2].

☐ We already practice this technique

☐ This technique would not be suitable for our operation

☐ We practiced this in the past and need to jumpstart

☐ We should implement this technique

Assigned to: _____

Projected Date of Implementation: _____

Technique #11

Assess Applicant Problem Solving Skills

During interviews, a technique should be used to gauge the problem-solving skills of frontline associates. One such technique entails showing the candidate a container filled with small items, such as paperclips, and asking how s/he would go about estimating the number of items in the container (without opening it).

☐ We already practice this technique

☐ This technique would not be suitable for our operation

☐ We practiced this in the past and need to jumpstart

☐ We should implement this technique

Assigned to: _____

Projected Date of Implementation: _____

Technique #12

Assess Applicant Innovativeness

On the application form for college students to intern at the hotel, ask the internship applicants to write a paragraph detailing a creative solution to a problem. For example: "Please describe one innovative solution to reducing guests' perceived waiting times at check-in."

- ☐ We already practice this technique
- ☐ This technique would not be suitable for our operation
- ☐ We practiced this in the past and need to jumpstart
- ☐ We should implement this technique

Assigned to: _____

Projected Date of Implementation: _____

Technique #13

Incorporate a Walk-Through During an Interview

As part of the interview process, walk the applicant around the job area and observe how s/he interacts with the employees as well as the guests. These observations provide a glimpse into the likely tone of interactions they will have if hired. In addition, when you let him/her see the work area and tasks, s/he may decide this is not a good fit or might become more excited about the prospect of working there.

- ☐ We already practice this technique
- ☐ This technique would not be suitable for our operation
- ☐ We practiced this in the past and need to jumpstart
- ☐ We should implement this technique

Assigned to: _____

Projected Date of Implementation: _____

Technique #14

Incorporate a Slideshow During an Interview

When interviewing a job candidate, if the interviewer is pleased with the performance of the candidate, the interviewer should complete the meeting by showing the candidate a slideshow on his/her laptop. The slideshow should include pictures of team members and pictures of them interacting. While viewing the pictures, stories can be shared regarding how the team members have been developed to be key players.

☐ We already practice this technique

☐ This technique would not be suitable for our operation

☐ We practiced this in the past and need to jumpstart

☐ We should implement this technique

Assigned to: _____

Projected Date of Implementation: _____

Technique #15

Reinforce Reputation During an Interview

When interviewing a job candidate, if the interviewer is pleased with the performance of the candidate, the interviewer should make a point of telling the applicant about some of the accolades won by the hotel, the brand, and/or the management company.

☐ We already practice this technique

☐ This technique would not be suitable for our operation

☐ We practiced this in the past and need to jumpstart

☐ We should implement this technique

Assigned to: _____

Projected Date of Implementation: _____

CHAPTER 2

Frontline Employee Training

Now that you have recruited and selected the best possible candidates, it is your responsibility to develop and educate them, so that they can perform at the highest level. With regard to training service skills, the basics of service and company culture need to be covered in a new

> "What if we train them and they leave? What if we don't... and they stay?"

employee orientation as early in employment as practically possible. This early orientation is needed because research indicates [3] that peer support is a key driver of how well-trained skills stick through time [4]. Therefore, if new associates display poor service skills because they are untrained, other associates who are trained will be less likely to display the skills.

Service skills must be reinforced and refined through the use of daily shift huddles. Daily shift huddles should be documented because they are more likely to occur and are more likely to be taken seriously with documentation. Key verbal and nonverbal customer service cues can be rotated through as huddle topics. The differences between on-stage and off-stage behaviors can also be discussed in the huddles.

Research indicates that guest surprises are key drivers of satisfaction. Specifically, a recent study found that when a blogger includes the word 'satisfied' when detailing his/her hotel experiences on a hotel review blog, then s/he is about 30 percent likely to recommend the hotel to a friend. If a blogger includes the phrase 'very satisfied' when detailing his/her hotel experiences on a hotel review blog, then s/he is approximately 60 percent likely to recommend the hotel to a friend. If, however, a blogger includes the phrase 'delightful surprise,' 'pleasant surprise,' 'excellent surprise,' or 'positive surprise' when detailing his/her hotel experiences on a hotel review blog, then s/he is approximately 97 percent likely to recommend the hotel to a friend [5]. Therefore, daily huddles can be used as tools to foster a culture in which associates will be motivated to surprise guests. That is, during shift huddles associates can be randomly called upon and asked to share a story with the group regarding how s/he has surprised a guest within the past couple of days.

Lastly, because adults learn through repetition, daily shift huddles can be concluded by reminding the group of one core value of the company. The values can be rotated; for example, if a company has eight core values then each one would be discussed every eighth day.

Technique #16

Ingrain the Ten Feet Rule

During new employee orientation, it must be emphasized to all new employees that they must greet guests whenever they pass within 10 feet of them. It is never acceptable to not greet a guest. If the guest is on his/her mobile phone then a smile, a nod, and a wave can serve as the greeting.

☐   We already practice this technique

☐   This technique would not be suitable for our operation

☐   We practiced this in the past and need to jumpstart

☐   We should implement this technique

Assigned to: _____

Projected Date of Implementation: _____

Technique #17

Help Employees to Remember Guest Names

During new employee orientation, everyone should be provided with some tactics regarding how to remember repeat guests' names.

☐   We already practice this technique

☐   This technique would not be suitable for our operation

☐   We practiced this in the past and need to jumpstart

☐   We should implement this technique

Assigned to: _____

Projected Date of Implementation: _____

Technique #18

Offer Body Language Training

During new employee orientation, all new frontline associates should be provided training regarding how to manage their body language cues when interacting with guests. Such cues include items such as smiling, eye contact, hands in pockets, etc.

☐ We already practice this technique

☐ This technique would not be suitable for our operation

☐ We practiced this in the past and need to jumpstart

☐ We should implement this technique

Assigned to: _____

Projected Date of Implementation: _____

Technique #19

Incorporate Surprise Stories in Shift Huddles

In every daily shift huddle, one associate should be randomly selected to tell the group how s/he positively surprised a guest in the past 48 hours.

☐ We already practice this technique

☐ This technique would not be suitable for our operation

☐ We practiced this in the past and need to jumpstart

☐ We should implement this technique

Assigned to: _____

Projected Date of Implementation: _____

Technique #20

Incorporate Encounter Stories in Shift Huddles

What guest did you meet today? In every daily shift huddle, one associate should be randomly selected to name a guest s/he met and tell the group something about the guest such as where they are from, their family, etc. This practice in the huddle will encourage the staff to talk to the guests.

☐   We already practice this technique

☐   This technique would not be suitable for our operation

☐   We practiced this in the past and need to jumpstart

☐   We should implement this technique

Assigned to: _____

Projected Date of Implementation: _____

Technique #21

Conduct a Core Value Rotation in Shift Huddles

Every hotel should have between 8–10 core values that define the organizational culture. At the end of each daily shift huddle, one of the core values should be discussed so that each one is covered in an 8–10 day rotation.

☐   We already practice this technique

☐   This technique would not be suitable for our operation

☐   We practiced this in the past and need to jumpstart

☐   We should implement this technique

Assigned to: _____

Projected Date of Implementation: _____

Technique #22

Incorporate Local Area Quizzes in Shift Huddles

At least once per week during a daily shift huddle, the associates present should be asked 2–3 questions about the local area (e.g., Does store XX open on Sundays? Where does the horse and carriage ride begin?)

☐   We already practice this technique

☐   This technique would not be suitable for our operation

☐   We practiced this in the past and need to jumpstart

☐   We should implement this technique

Assigned to: _____

Projected Date of Implementation: _____

Technique #23

Use Foreign Language Greetings When Appropriate

In hotel properties with an international clientele, the front desk agents should know greetings in various languages and use them when appropriate.

- ☐ We already practice this technique
- ☐ This technique would not be suitable for our operation
- ☐ We practiced this in the past and need to jumpstart
- ☐ We should implement this technique

Assigned to: _____

Projected Date of Implementation: _____

Technique #24

Ingrain the Drama Metaphor

All associates should be taught that they are on-stage whenever a guest can see or hear him/her. Such on-stage behavior applies to associates regardless of whether or not they are clocked-in for work. In other words, a guest perceives a uniformed employee as a representative of the hotel whether the employee has begun his/her shift or not.

☐ We already practice this technique

☐ This technique would not be suitable for our operation

☐ We practiced this in the past and need to jumpstart

☐ We should implement this technique

Assigned to: _____

Projected Date of Implementation: _____

Technique #25

Train the 'Again' Effect

If an associate recognizes a guest as being a repeat patron, but cannot recall his/her name, the associate should be trained to say 'nice to see you *again.*' Inserting the word 'again' helps strengthen the relationship between the guest and service provider.

☐ We already practice this technique

☐ This technique would not be suitable for our operation

☐ We practiced this in the past and need to jumpstart

☐ We should implement this technique

Assigned to: _____

Projected Date of Implementation: _____

Technique #26

Express Gratitude to Guests

A guest must feel appreciated and cannot be thanked too much. Associates should be trained to thank them for their business throughout their stay: "Thank you for staying with us", "Thank you for dining with us", etc.

- ☐ We already practice this technique
- ☐ This technique would not be suitable for our operation
- ☐ We practiced this in the past and need to jumpstart
- ☐ We should implement this technique

Assigned to: _____

Projected Date of Implementation: _____

Technique #27

Teach Proper Response to 'Thank You'

All associates should be trained to reply with 'thank you' when a guest says 'thank you'. Intense competition in the hotel sector mandates that guests feel appreciated for their business. Replies to 'thank you' such as 'no problem' do not communicate appreciation or leave a lasting impression.

☐   We already practice this technique

☐   This technique would not be suitable for our operation

☐   We practiced this in the past and need to jumpstart

☐   We should implement this technique

Assigned to: _____

Projected Date of Implementation: _____

Technique #28

Set the Tone During the Reservation Process

When a guest makes a reservation via the hotel, it creates a great opportunity to get them excited about coming to the hotel. The tone of the reservationist's voice is very important and has the opportunity to start the exceptional guest service before they even arrive at the hotel. Reservationists should be trained to speak with enthusiasm, so the guest will feel it too. This enthusiasm sets the tone for their stay.

☐ We already practice this technique

☐ This technique would not be suitable for our operation

☐ We practiced this in the past and need to jumpstart

☐ We should implement this technique

Assigned to: _____

Projected Date of Implementation: _____

Technique #29

Smile While on the Telephone

A mirror should be hung in front of all hotel reservationists and they should be trained to check their smiles in the mirror when conversing with potential guests. Smiling changes voice tone and inflection.

☐   We already practice this technique

☐   This technique would not be suitable for our operation

☐   We practiced this in the past and need to jumpstart

☐   We should implement this technique

Assigned to: _____

Projected Date of Implementation: _____

Technique #30

Do Not Unnecessarily Disclose Overbooking

Reservationists should be trained never to tell guests that they are overbooked on a requested night. Simply stating that the hotel is full would suffice in the conversation. Overbooking is viewed by many consumers as an unethical and greedy practice.

- ☐ We already practice this technique
- ☐ This technique would not be suitable for our operation
- ☐ We practiced this in the past and need to jumpstart
- ☐ We should implement this technique

Assigned to: _____

Projected Date of Implementation: _____

Technique #31

Use Hospitable Responses to 'How are you?'

If an associate is asked by a guest 'how are you?' the associate should not respond that s/he is happy because s/he is 'off tomorrow.' Expressing happiness because of an upcoming separation from guests does not communicate a hospitable culture.

☐ We already practice this technique

☐ This technique would not be suitable for our operation

☐ We practiced this in the past and need to jumpstart

☐ We should implement this technique

Assigned to: _____

Projected Date of Implementation: _____

Technique #32

Tell Jokes and Riddles to Children When Appropriate

All frontline associates should be instructed to learn at least one children's riddle that can be told when children move through their areas accompanied by their parents. A basic Internet search reveals numerous websites listing children's jokes and riddles.

☐ We already practice this technique

☐ This technique would not be suitable for our operation

☐ We practiced this in the past and need to jumpstart

☐ We should implement this technique

Assigned to: _____

Projected Date of Implementation: _____

Technique #33

Use Strong Telephone Greetings

An associate's name is important to a guest. All associates should be trained to state their names when they answer the telephones in their departments.

☐ We already practice this technique

☐ This technique would not be suitable for our operation

☐ We practiced this in the past and need to jumpstart

☐ We should implement this technique

Assigned to: _____

Projected Date of Implementation: _____

Technique #34

Make Guests the First Priority

Who's more important, the manager or the guest? The entire management team should understand that when an employee is engaged with a guest, the guest is most important. Likewise, some employees think that "Oh there is a manager, I better acknowledge him/her." Both management and staff should be taught to focus on the guest first.

☐ We already practice this technique

☐ This technique would not be suitable for our operation

☐ We practiced this in the past and need to jumpstart

☐ We should implement this technique

Assigned to: _____

Projected Date of Implementation: _____

Technique #35

Check Websites for Accuracy

During off-peak times, front desk associates should be trained to routinely check websites that describe the hotel for accuracy. Are the hours of operations correct for the various departments? Are the hotel's features and amenities listed correctly?

☐ We already practice this technique

☐ This technique would not be suitable for our operation

☐ We practiced this in the past and need to jumpstart

☐ We should implement this technique

Assigned to: _____

Projected Date of Implementation: _____

Technique #36

Learn the Language of Guest Segments

Do you know who your guests are? If you are near a university, medical center, or in a leisure market—bring in "specialists" to talk and train the hotel staff on what to say, ask and explain. These specialists normally will do it free of charge. The more knowledge your staff has, the easier it is to provide a more personalized style of service.

☐ We already practice this technique

☐ This technique would not be suitable for our operation

☐ We practiced this in the past and need to jumpstart

☐ We should implement this technique

Assigned to: _____

Projected Date of Implementation: _____

Technique #37

Eliminate Hairs

All housekeepers should be trained that the most common cleanliness problem in the guestroom experience is hair in the bathroom (on floor, tub, or vanity).

☐ We already practice this technique

☐ This technique would not be suitable for our operation

☐ We practiced this in the past and need to jumpstart

☐ We should implement this technique

Assigned to: _____

Projected Date of Implementation: _____

Technique #38

Offer Luggage Assistance

All hotel staff should be trained to spot guests carrying bags and to tell the guests that they would like to help carry the items for them. If the guests decline, the service offered signals care and attention to detail.

☐ We already practice this technique

☐ This technique would not be suitable for our operation

☐ We practiced this in the past and need to jumpstart

☐ We should implement this technique

Assigned to: _____

Projected Date of Implementation: _____

CHAPTER 3

Frontline Employee Feedback and Evaluation

In a management context, perhaps no writings illustrate the importance of feedback better than Spencer Johnson and Ken Blanchard's book titled the *One Minute Manager* [6] that was published more than thirty years ago. The sale of 13 million copies [7] is proof of the valuable message that is important to tell: human beings crave feedback.

> *All feedback...even constructive...can be more motivational than no feedback at all.*

A rookie supervisor who is too intimidated by his/her team to provide regular and substantive feedback is demotivating for those on the team who strive for excellence. Similarly, a veteran supervisor who has grown withdrawn and complacent through the years can be equally demotivating. The proper design and use of feedback is the backbone of a well-managed team. The word 'team' is purposefully used throughout this paragraph because the word allows for a useful analogy: Take a moment to imagine a soccer or football team whose coaching staff does not offer the players feedback regarding how to improve (i.e., coaching); how would the team perform? The answer is obvious.

As we know, feedback and evaluation can come in many forms in a hotel. Verbal feedback can and should be offered everyday. If you see someone on your team do something well, then tell him/her that it was done well... If you see someone on your team do something poorly, then tell them him/her that it was done poorly, and also provide the education and tools so that it can be done better in the next attempt.

With regard to written evaluations, as suggested by the techniques in this chapter, the standard form on which to complete all associates' written performance evaluations should contain a section evaluating customer service. While large hotel management firms have likely already adopted this practice, it is our understanding that there are many small regional management firms as well as independent hotel operators that may not include a section of customer service feedback on all written evaluation forms. In fact, some of these small players do not even use written evaluation forms. It is the sections of the form and the priorities and goals tailored for each associate through the use of the form that help create and reinforce a culture of excellence. It is this culture of excellence that ultimately translates into high guest satisfaction and loyalty. This culture of excellence is completely independent of a hotel's scale. That is, the proper use of feedback and evaluation can be used to foster service excellence just as easily in an economy brand as in a luxury brand.

Technique #39

Incorporate Service Assessment in Performance Evaluations

The standard form on which to complete all associates' written performance evaluations should contain a section evaluating customer service. For back-of-the-house employees, items such as teamwork and dependability can be addressed in this section as these items impact guest satisfaction scores.

☐ We already practice this technique

☐ This technique would not be suitable for our operation

☐ We practiced this in the past and need to jumpstart

☐ We should implement this technique

Assigned to: _____

Projected Date of Implementation: _____

Technique #40

Mystery Shop Telephone Etiquette

Hotel associates' telephone habits and etiquette should be shopped at least once per quarter. Are the hotel's telephones answered promptly? Does the hotel representative identify himself/herself by name? Is the reservationist enthusiastic?

☐   We already practice this technique

☐   This technique would not be suitable for our operation

☐   We practiced this in the past and need to jumpstart

☐   We should implement this technique

Assigned to: _____

Projected Date of Implementation: _____

Technique #41

Offer a Balance of Positive Feedback

Managers and supervisors cannot be complacent and must give constructive feedback whenever needed. Therefore, in an effort to avoid being perceived a negative or a 'nitpicker,' each manager or supervisor should not go home for the day without giving at least six positive pieces of feedback to associates (e.g., "your shoes are nicely polished;" "I like the way you phrased that response to the guest inquiry," etc.).

❏ We already practice this technique

❏ This technique would not be suitable for our operation

❏ We practiced this in the past and need to jumpstart

❏ We should implement this technique

Assigned to: _____

Projected Date of Implementation: _____

Technique #42

Mystery Shop Customer Service

The hotel should use one mystery shopper guest every quarter to evaluate customer service at the various hotel/guest points of contact. In some quarters, the mystery shopper should be disguised as a business traveler and in other quarters, the mystery shopper should be accompanied by a friend and be under the guise of a leisure traveler.

☐ We already practice this technique

☐ This technique would not be suitable for our operation

☐ We practiced this in the past and need to jumpstart

☐ We should implement this technique

Assigned to: _____

Projected Date of Implementation: _____

Technique #43

Set Cross-Training Goals

In the section of the associate performance evaluation in which goals are set, all associates should have at least one goal related to being cross-trained on a new area within his/her department or in a different department.

☐ We already practice this technique

☐ This technique would not be suitable for our operation

☐ We practiced this in the past and need to jumpstart

☐ We should implement this technique

Assigned to: _____

Projected Date of Implementation: _____

Technique #44

Allow for Self-Assigned Goals

In the section of the performance evaluation in which goals are set for the associate, s/he should be permitted to set at least one goal for himself/herself. The associate needs ownership and buy-in on the goals.

☐ We already practice this technique

☐ This technique would not be suitable for our operation

☐ We practiced this in the past and need to jumpstart

☐ We should implement this technique

Assigned to: _____

Projected Date of Implementation: _____

1	2	3	4	5	6	7	8	9	10
11	12	13	14	15	16	17	18	19	20
21	22	23	24	25	26	27	28	29	30
31	32	33	34	35	36	37	38	39	40
41	42	43	44	__45__	__46__	__47__	__48__	__49__	__50__
__51__	__52__	__53__	__54__	__55__	__56__	__57__	__58__	__59__	__60__
__61__	__62__	__63__	__64__	__65__	__66__	__67__	__68__	__69__	__70__
__71__	__72__	__73__	__74__	__75__	__76__	__77__	__78__	__79__	__80__
__81__	__82__	__83__	__84__	__85__	__86__	__87__	__88__	__89__	__90__
__91__	__92__	__93__	__94__	__95__	__96__	__97__	__98__	__99__	__100__
__101__	__102__	__103__	__104__	__105__	__106__	__107__	__108__	__109__	__110__
__111__	__112__	__113__	__114__	__115__	__116__	__117__	__118__	__119__	__120__
__121__	__122__	__123__	__124__	__125__	__126__	__127__	__128__	__129__	__130__
__131__	__132__	__133__	__134__	__135__	__136__	__137__	__138__	139	140
141	142	143	144	145	146	147	148	149	150
151	152	153	154	155	156	157	158	159	160
161	162	163	164	165	166	167	168	169	170
171	172	173	174	175	176	177	178	179	180
181	182	183	184	185	186	187	188	189	

A Hotel Manager's Handbook

Section II

• • • • • • • • • • • • • • • •

Delivering the Service Experience

PREVIEW

Now associates are selected and trained, and the guests are on property. This section offers techniques for maximizing satisfaction at various interaction points. The many guest-associate interfaces, in comparison to other service industries (such as, restaurant or retail), offer hoteliers many opportunities to shine as well as many opportunities to mess up. This section offers ammunition to shine.

CHAPTER 4

The Check-In Experience

Malcolm Gladwell's well-known book titled *Blink: The Power of Thinking Without Thinking* [8] reinforces the emphasis that consumers place upon first impressions. Gladwell explains that consumers often practice what is termed 'thin-slicing' in which they assess situations based upon small windows of information.

"There can be as much value in the blink of an eye as in months of rational analysis."

—*Malcolm Gladwell*

Such thin-slicing applies to the psychological emphasis that is afforded to the hotel check-in experience. Through the lens of the guest, both verbal and nonverbal cues that guests are exposed to during the check-in experience serve as signals of the impending lodging experience. If the check-in experience is sub-par then the negative emotions generated in the guest's mind often carry over as a halo effect to influence judgments of other hotel facets and amenities. By halo effect, we are referring to the ability of impressions made in one area to carry-over and influence impressions in another area [9]. Whether, rational or irrational, whether justifiable or not, the first impressions made at check-in do influence guest's impressions and judgments in other areas.

Why does the halo effect carry first impressions made at the front desk to other facets of the hotel experience? Are guests really this irrational?

To state that guests are irrational might be a bit unfair. The fact of the matter, however, is that throughout the course of the 20th century social scientists have identified and documented a number of biases in human reasoning. One such bias in human reasoning is termed confirmatory bias which supports the notion that individuals often unknowingly misinterpret new information in an effort to confirm or support previously formulated perceptions [10]. It is this confirmatory bias that lays the foundation for the halo effect that the check-in experience imparts over subsequent facets of the hotel experience.

Due to the importance of the check-in experience, this chapter provides a number of techniques for delivering high-quality first impressions. Some techniques focus on verbal cues and other on non-verbal cues, but when used in combination, these techniques can foster a front desk culture in which strong and hospitable first impressions are the norm.

Technique #45

Use Strong Verbal Greetings at Check-In

A front desk associate should never address a guest with the phrase 'checking in?' Such a greeting does not engender a spirit of hospitality. Would an initial greeting to a visiting friend at your home be 'staying with me?'

☐ We already practice this technique

☐ This technique would not be suitable for our operation

☐ We practiced this in the past and need to jumpstart

☐ We should implement this technique

Assigned to: _____

Projected Date of Implementation: _____

Technique #46

Eliminate the View of Employee Trashcans

A trashcan does not engender a sense of hospitality. Trashcans used behind the front desk should be positioned so that guests cannot see them.

☐   We already practice this technique

☐   This technique would not be suitable for our operation

☐   We practiced this in the past and need to jumpstart

☐   We should implement this technique

Assigned to: _____

Projected Date of Implementation: _____

Technique #47

Offer Infused Water at Check-In

· ·

During prime check-in hours, keep a beverage dispenser of infused water in the lobby area. Guests can be instructed to help themselves to the water that can be infused with flavors such as strawberry or cucumber.

❑   We already practice this technique

❑   This technique would not be suitable for our operation

❑   We practiced this in the past and need to jumpstart

❑   We should implement this technique

Assigned to: _____

Projected Date of Implementation: _____

Technique #48

Dispense Information on Tour Bus

If your hotel has tour buses staying at the hotel, have a representative get on the bus before the guests disembark. The hotel representative will have an opportunity to welcome the guests to the hotel, explain outlet hours, and any pertinent information regarding their stay. If they have to wait in line to give a credit card, they can be instructed at this time. Once they enter the hotel you will lose the "togetherness" of the group.

☐   We already practice this technique

☐   This technique would not be suitable for our operation

☐   We practiced this in the past and need to jumpstart

☐   We should implement this technique

Assigned to: _____

Projected Date of Implementation: _____

Technique #49

Designate a Children's Check-In Spot

If a significant number of family check-ins are expected on a given day, designate a spot at the front desk with a sign reading 'children's check-in' and place a step-stool at the spot so that children can see over the front desk. As a component of the children's check-in, the child could be asked if s/he would like to provide a signature on a document. Such a signature request might be the first time the child has ever been asked for his/her signature.

☐ We already practice this technique

☐ This technique would not be suitable for our operation

☐ We practiced this in the past and need to jumpstart

☐ We should implement this technique

Assigned to: _____

Projected Date of Implementation: _____

Technique #50

Use High Quality Pens at the Front Desk

Always have an ample supply of high-quality pens at the front desk for guests to use while checking-in. At least one person per group must physically touch the pen. The use of a high-quality pen is a subconscious signal of attention to detail.

☐ We already practice this technique

☐ This technique would not be suitable for our operation

☐ We practiced this in the past and need to jumpstart

☐ We should implement this technique

Assigned to: _____

Projected Date of Implementation: _____

Technique #51

Incorporate a Guessing Game for Children

Keep a cardboard box with a hole in it behind the front desk. When a child is checking-in with parents, if the front desk is not too busy, ask the child if s/he would like to feel inside the hole and guess what the box contains. If the child guesses correctly, then s/he wins a prize. Unique objects such as a pine cone can be the touch-item in the box. Prizes can be small trinkets ordered from a vendor such as Oriental Trading Company. Or, a series of three boxes can be set-up and if the child guesses all three items correctly then s/he can be issued a certificate.

- ☐ We already practice this technique
- ☐ This technique would not be suitable for our operation
- ☐ We practiced this in the past and need to jumpstart
- ☐ We should implement this technique

Assigned to: _____

Projected Date of Implementation: _____

Technique #52

Offer a Pet

When a child is checking-in with parents, ask the child if she brought a pet. When she says 'no' ask her if she would like a pet for the duration of her stay. When she says 'yes' then let her pick a fish from a fish tank and put it in a fish bowl in her guestroom.

- ☐ We already practice this technique
- ☐ This technique would not be suitable for our operation
- ☐ We practiced this in the past and need to jumpstart
- ☐ We should implement this technique

Assigned to: _____

Projected Date of Implementation: _____

Technique #53

Have Word Search Puzzles and Coloring Sheets at the Front Desk

Welcome the children checking in as well as the adults. Surprise them with a word search puzzle or coloring page directly relating to your hotel. Such items occupy the child's time as well as make them feel welcome.

❑   We already practice this technique

❑   This technique would not be suitable for our operation

❑   We practiced this in the past and need to jumpstart

❑   We should implement this technique

Assigned to: _____

Projected Date of Implementation: _____

Technique #54

Offer a Sticker Treasure Hunt

At check-in, young children can be given sticker books. They can collect more stickers for the books by either visiting various locations around the hotel or by visiting local attractions. This effort, in essence, serves as a treasure hunt by means of the sticker book.

❏ We already practice this technique

❏ This technique would not be suitable for our operation

❏ We practiced this in the past and need to jumpstart

❏ We should implement this technique

Assigned to: _____

Projected Date of Implementation: _____

Technique #55

Host a Nutella Party

On a day with a large number of family check-ins, a sign can be placed at the front desk announcing an evening Nutella party for the children.

❑ We already practice this technique

❑ This technique would not be suitable for our operation

❑ We practiced this in the past and need to jumpstart

❑ We should implement this technique

Assigned to: _____

Projected Date of Implementation: _____

Technique #56

Offer a Dog Training Class for Children

If someone on the management team has a well-trained dog, then s/he can periodically place a sign in the lobby reading 'Dog Training Class at 4:00 PM.' The manager can bring his/her dog and demonstrate some of the commands that the dog knows for the children.

☐ We already practice this technique

☐ This technique would not be suitable for our operation

☐ We practiced this in the past and need to jumpstart

☐ We should implement this technique

Assigned to: _____

Projected Date of Implementation: _____

 *Technique #57*

Allow Guests the Opportunity to Jog with Members of the Management Team

At check-in, guests can be invited to go on a group jog with a member of the hotel's management team at a set time in the A.M. The group jog can occur every morning by rotating the responsibility between several members of the management team who enjoy jogging. Conversations during the jog will help solidify bonds between the hotel and guests.

☐ We already practice this technique

☐ This technique would not be suitable for our operation

☐ We practiced this in the past and need to jumpstart

☐ We should implement this technique

Assigned to: _____

Projected Date of Implementation: _____

Technique #58

Roll Out the Red Carpet

Periodically roll out a red carpet near the entrance of the hotel (or inside the lobby leading to the front desk). Management can be creative with the signage which can read "Welcome to *Hotel X*, where red carpet treatment is the norm" or "Red carpet treatment at a value."

☐   We already practice this technique

☐   This technique would not be suitable for our operation

☐   We practiced this in the past and need to jumpstart

☐   We should implement this technique

Assigned to: _____

Projected Date of Implementation: _____

Technique #59

Offer Treat Bags for Pets

How you treat a guest's pet is very important. If a guest pays for a pet to stay at a hotel, then the pet is likely considered a member of the family. Create a treat bag, distributed at check-in, which contains a treat, directions on where to take the pet to go out, a poop bag, and the "rules" for the pet room.

❑ We already practice this technique

❑ This technique would not be suitable for our operation

❑ We practiced this in the past and need to jumpstart

❑ We should implement this technique

Assigned to: _____

Projected Date of Implementation: _____

Technique #60

Remember Pet Names

Front desk agents should be taught to record pet names in the guest history section of the property management system. Along with the pet's name, the agent should also insert a short (3–4 words) physical description of the pet. When the pet revisits, s/he should be addressed by name.

☐ We already practice this technique

☐ This technique would not be suitable for our operation

☐ We practiced this in the past and need to jumpstart

☐ We should implement this technique

Assigned to: _____

Projected Date of Implementation: _____

Technique #61

Offer Aromatherapy

If a guest mentions that s/he is stressed for any reason (e.g., travel or work frustrations), offer him/her a plug-in aromatherapy treatment that can be used in the guestroom to relieve stress.

☐ We already practice this technique

☐ This technique would not be suitable for our operation

☐ We practiced this in the past and need to jumpstart

☐ We should implement this technique

Assigned to: _____

Projected Date of Implementation: _____

Technique #62

Offer Free Upgrades on Occasion

If a guest mentions that s/he is stressed for any reason (e.g., travel or work frustrations), offer him/her a complimentary upgrade to a suite-style room (if available).

☐   We already practice this technique

☐   This technique would not be suitable for our operation

☐   We practiced this in the past and need to jumpstart

☐   We should implement this technique

Assigned to: _____

Projected Date of Implementation: _____

Technique #63

'Google Image' Guests with Unique Names

If a front desk agent has some downtime between tasks, then s/he should be taught to search the arrival list for guests who have visited in the past and who have unique names (e.g., Vincent Magnini). The agent can then "Google Image" those names so that the guest can be greeted by name upon arrival.

☐ We already practice this technique

☐ This technique would not be suitable for our operation

☐ We practiced this in the past and need to jumpstart

☐ We should implement this technique

Assigned to: _____

Projected Date of Implementation: _____

Technique #64

Create a Strategic Alliance with a Car Wash

The hotel could establish a strategic alliance with a mobile waterless car wash provider. Each front desk associate can be empowered to select one incoming guest each day and ask them if s/he would like a complimentary exterior car detailing during their stay. Conversely, the 10th guest checking in every day could be made the complimentary offer to help ensure fairness.

☐ We already practice this technique

☐ This technique would not be suitable for our operation

☐ We practiced this in the past and need to jumpstart

☐ We should implement this technique

Assigned to: _____

Projected Date of Implementation: _____

Technique #65

Record Guests' Preferences

Repeat guests want to be recognized. Frontline staff should utilize the computer system to keep information on the guest's desires such as room type, location, favorite drink, etc.

❏   We already practice this technique

❏   This technique would not be suitable for our operation

❏   We practiced this in the past and need to jumpstart

❏   We should implement this technique

Assigned to: _____

Projected Date of Implementation: _____

Technique #66

Drive Bookings to the Proprietary Website

If a front desk agent sees that a regular guest is using a 3rd party OTA to book his/her room, the agent should inform the guest that equivalent rates can be found on the hotel's proprietary site. It should be explained that the savings in fees and commissions by the hotel would be used for additional guest services and amenities.

❏   We already practice this technique

❏   This technique would not be suitable for our operation

❏   We practiced this in the past and need to jumpstart

❏   We should implement this technique

Assigned to: _____

Projected Date of Implementation: _____

CHAPTER 5

The Guestroom Experience

Even if only for a night, the sleeping room is the guest's home away from home. Traveling, whether for business or leisure, is tiring. The sleeping room is the space in which rejuvenation occurs—a place where batteries are recharged. The role of the hotel is to understand the guest well enough so that the hotel's resources can be used in the best possible means to foster this warm, rejuvenating environment.

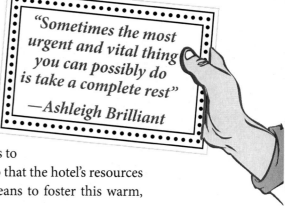

"Sometimes the most urgent and vital thing you can possibly do is take a complete rest"
—Ashleigh Brilliant

Relating these discussions to guest satisfaction, why is it that if all hotel rooms offer similar products (e.g., a bed, a commode, a shower) some properties consistently achieve high guest satisfaction ratings while others consistently record poor ratings? Are these ratings a function of the quality of the bed, commode, and shower? If so, then why is it that an economy hotel with a $109 ADR can attain higher guest satisfaction ratings than an upscale property with a $219 ADR?

A customer satisfaction typology developed by Professor Noriaki Kano in the 1980s can be used to shed light on some of the above questions [11]. According to Kano's model, there are some facets of a service offering that are expected by all customers as norms and, therefore, do not have an upside satisfaction potential. For example, it is unlikely that guests will rate a sleeping room higher if it has a secure lock on the door, but will rate it lower if the lock in not functioning properly. Such a feature that will not increase satisfaction scores when present, but will decrease when absent, is termed a *must-be* attribute according to Kano's model. *Must-be* attributes are commonly accepted as things that hotels get right and there is not much variation in performance on these items and, consequently, guests have grown to expect them through time and take them for granted.

On the other hand, other features of the guestroom such as bathroom cleanliness can drive satisfaction ratings up or down depending upon performance. A search of the phrase 'bathroom cleanliness' or more specific phrases such as 'hair on floor' or 'dirty tub' on a site such as Trip Advisor reveal it is not easy to keep bathrooms consistently clean for guests—managing both the ability and motivation of a housekeeping staff requires knowledge and experience. Due to variations in performance on such dimensions, termed one-dimensions in Kano's model, positive performance drive satisfaction scores up and negative performance pulls them down.

In a hotel guestroom, there are also what Kano's model terms *attractive* attributes which increase satisfaction if present, but do not decrease satisfaction if absent. These attractive attributes are items that take the guest by surprise. Because the physical features of a hotel room can be examined online prior to the hotel experience, these surprise items often involve actions of the staff—for example, an attentive housekeeper delivering something unexpected.

In order to deliver a high-quality guestroom experience, hoteliers must understand how to manage each facet of Kano's model. Consequently, the techniques presented in this chapter address each.

Technique #67

Use Solid White Bed Linens

All bed linens and bed coverings, including the foot scarf and pillow shams, should be solid white. A solid white bed subconsciously signals cleanliness and spaciousness.

☐ We already practice this technique

☐ This technique would not be suitable for our operation

☐ We practiced this in the past and need to jumpstart

☐ We should implement this technique

Assigned to: _____

Projected Date of Implementation: _____

Technique #68

Place a Follow-Up Call

After the guest checks in, the front desk clerk (or another desired employee) should call the guestroom to see if everything meets the guest's expectations. This person should give the guest their name and instruct them to call them if anything is desired.

- ☐ We already practice this technique
- ☐ This technique would not be suitable for our operation
- ☐ We practiced this in the past and need to jumpstart
- ☐ We should implement this technique

Assigned to: _____

Projected Date of Implementation: _____

Technique #69

Have Different Color Towels Available

Have different color towel sets available upon request for groups of friends staying together who do not want to get their towels mixed up. These colored towel sets can also be available upon request if someone in a traveling family has a cold and wants to minimize the risk of spreading germs to other members of the family.

☐ We already practice this technique

☐ This technique would not be suitable for our operation

☐ We practiced this in the past and need to jumpstart

☐ We should implement this technique

Assigned to: _____

Projected Date of Implementation: _____

Technique #70

Encourage Guests to Take Hangers Home

Rather than affixing clothes hangers to the clothing rod so that guests cannot depart with them, take the opposite strategy and invite guests to keep a hanger. Ask a local art studio or vendor to creatively decorate the hangers to include the name/logo of the hotel and the name/logo of the art studio. Such decorated hangers placed in the guest's residence closet at home are good brand reinforcement for both the hotel and studio.

☐ We already practice this technique

☐ This technique would not be suitable for our operation

☐ We practiced this in the past and need to jumpstart

☐ We should implement this technique

Assigned to: _____

Projected Date of Implementation: _____

Technique #71

Display Towel Animals

When refreshing a room, if a housekeeper detects that a family with a child is occupying the room then s/he should fold one of the guestroom towels into an animal formation. Straightforward instructions for basic animal designs can be found on YouTube.

- ☐ We already practice this technique
- ☐ This technique would not be suitable for our operation
- ☐ We practiced this in the past and need to jumpstart
- ☐ We should implement this technique

Assigned to: _____

Projected Date of Implementation: _____

Technique #72

Have a Celebrity Make Your Wake-Up Calls

As a surprise tactic, ask a well-known celebrity or comedian to prerecord the wake-up call message that is used in the hotel.

☐ We already practice this technique

☐ This technique would not be suitable for our operation

☐ We practiced this in the past and need to jumpstart

☐ We should implement this technique

Assigned to: _____

Projected Date of Implementation: _____

Technique #73

Have Surprise Amenity Bags Available

Do guests ask or "take" your amenities such as shampoo, lotion, or soap? If so, take what can be a negative and turn it into a positive. Have some amenity bags made of the basic amenities in a small mesh type bag. When a guest asks for some, present them with this and see if they would like it. What a nice surprise "gift" it will be and since you would be giving them the product anyway, for a few cents more, it exceeds their expectations.

☐ We already practice this technique

☐ This technique would not be suitable for our operation

☐ We practiced this in the past and need to jumpstart

☐ We should implement this technique

Assigned to: _____

Projected Date of Implementation: _____

Technique #74

Send Surprises to Rooms

Every front desk agent should be empowered to pick two guestrooms per shift to target with a surprise amenity. The surprise amenity should be an item indigenous to the local area such as a slice of key lime pie in Key West.

- ☐ We already practice this technique
- ☐ This technique would not be suitable for our operation
- ☐ We practiced this in the past and need to jumpstart
- ☐ We should implement this technique

Assigned to: _____

Projected Date of Implementation: _____

Technique #75

Recognize Special Events

If a guest mentions a birthday, anniversary, wedding, or other celebratory event either at check-in or at the time of reservation, surprise him/her with a bottle of champagne or something special with a notecard with your information. The guest will remember this forever.

☐ We already practice this technique

☐ This technique would not be suitable for our operation

☐ We practiced this in the past and need to jumpstart

☐ We should implement this technique

Assigned to: _____

Projected Date of Implementation: _____

Technique #76

Offer Photo Opportunities for Guests

Place a note in the room stating that the guest(s) can stop by the front desk at any time and an agent will take a photo of the guest(s) in the lobby and the photo will be placed on the holiday card that the guest(s) receives from the hotel. In addition, a past photo of the guest can be placed in a frame on the nightstand before the guest arrives. If these photos can be uploaded into the property management system then they can be used to help the front desk agents memorize the names of the regulars.

☐ We already practice this technique

☐ This technique would not be suitable for our operation

☐ We practiced this in the past and need to jumpstart

☐ We should implement this technique

Assigned to: _____

Projected Date of Implementation: _____

Technique #77

Have Occupation Costumes Available

If a telephone reservation is being made for a family with a young child, then the agent can ask the parent making the reservation if the child would like an occupation costume in the guestroom upon arrival. The agent can list the costumes that the hotel has and let the parent indicate the most suitable one (e.g., doctor, veterinarian, firefighter, etc.).

❑ We already practice this technique

❑ This technique would not be suitable for our operation

❑ We practiced this in the past and need to jumpstart

❑ We should implement this technique

Assigned to: _____

Projected Date of Implementation: _____

Technique #78

Surprise Toddlers with Bath Toys

If accommodations are being used by a family with a toddler, housekeeping can place an unopened package of bath toys in the room.

☐   We already practice this technique

☐   This technique would not be suitable for our operation

☐   We practiced this in the past and need to jumpstart

☐   We should implement this technique

Assigned to: _____

Projected Date of Implementation: _____

Technique #79

Pose Stuffed Animals in Fun Positions

When servicing a room with children and there are stuffed animals or something similar, the housekeeper should make it look fun by putting the animals in clear view of the bed in a way that will be enjoyable for the child to see when s/he returns to the room.

☐ We already practice this technique

☐ This technique would not be suitable for our operation

☐ We practiced this in the past and need to jumpstart

☐ We should implement this technique

Assigned to: _____

Projected Date of Implementation: _____

Technique #80

Encourage Postcard Usage

Place a postcard with a picture of the hotel on the guestroom desk. The postcard should be stamped with prepaid postage.

☐ We already practice this technique

☐ This technique would not be suitable for our operation

☐ We practiced this in the past and need to jumpstart

☐ We should implement this technique

Assigned to: _____

Projected Date of Implementation: _____

Technique #81

Surprise Guests with Personalized Candy

Every week strategically select 10–20 incoming guests from the centralized reservation system and order candy wrappers personalized with their names. Place the personalized candy in their rooms during their stay. Alternatively, at a bare minimum, have candy on hand with customized wrappers displaying the hotel name/logo.

❑ We already practice this technique

❑ This technique would not be suitable for our operation

❑ We practiced this in the past and need to jumpstart

❑ We should implement this technique

Assigned to: _____

Projected Date of Implementation: _____

Technique #82

Replace Old Coffeemakers

If in-room coffeemakers with glass carafes are still being used, they should be replaced with coffeemakers that drip directly into the drinking cup.

☐ We already practice this technique

☐ This technique would not be suitable for our operation

☐ We practiced this in the past and need to jumpstart

☐ We should implement this technique

Assigned to: _____

Projected Date of Implementation: _____

Technique #83

Review In-Room Information for Accuracy

At least once per quarter, hotel management or staff should check that the information in the in-room hotel information book is up-to-date and accurate.

☐ We already practice this technique

☐ This technique would not be suitable for our operation

☐ We practiced this in the past and need to jumpstart

☐ We should implement this technique

Assigned to: _____

Projected Date of Implementation: _____

Technique #84

Check Telephone Labeling for Accuracy

At least twice per year, the buttons on the telephones in the guestrooms should be checked for labeling accuracy.

☐   We already practice this technique

☐   This technique would not be suitable for our operation

☐   We practiced this in the past and need to jumpstart

☐   We should implement this technique

Assigned to: _____

Projected Date of Implementation: _____

Technique #85

Offer to Name a Room After a Frequent Guest

If a guest stays at your property more than 50 nights per year, then offer to name a guestroom in honor of him/her. A small plaque can be displayed in the room or corridor.

☐ We already practice this technique

☐ This technique would not be suitable for our operation

☐ We practiced this in the past and need to jumpstart

☐ We should implement this technique

Assigned to: _____

Projected Date of Implementation: _____

CHAPTER 6

The Public Space Experience

Atmospherics in the public spaces—the management of all five senses—play a large part in shaping the guest experience. For example: touch cues can be managed by providing clean and comfortable seating; site cues can be managed by providing clean and uncluttered lines of vision; audio cues can be managed by airing the appropriate music at the appropriate volume; olfactory cues can be managed through the use of ambient scents; taste cues can be managed by providing seasonal food or beverage tastings in the lobby.

> *"Consciousness plays only a small role in our experiences 'about the size of a snowball on top of an iceberg'"*
>
> —*Timothy*

The management of all five sense perceptions influences guests on a subconscious level as they move through the hotel's public spaces. The proper use of atmospheric cues subconsciously improves moods and emotional states. *Subconscious* is the key word here because it is unlikely that a guest will state that s/he is in a good mood because jazz music is playing or because the hotel lobby is scented—these cues typically trigger responses without guests consciously realizing the effects.

Searching in sites such as Trip Advisor confirms that guests rarely state that they enjoy atmospheric cues such as music or scents in hotel public spaces (they do not think to make such comments due to the subconscious nature of the cues). Nevertheless, scientific studies that experimentally manipulate the cues do confirm the power of such elements in influencing both moods and emotions.

One atmospheric cue that deserves particular attention is cleanliness. The old adage that states that the cleanliness of a restaurant's restroom is a signal of kitchen cleanliness holds true in the context of hotel public space discussions as well. If an empty Starbuck's cup is left on an end table in a hotel's public space, the length of time that it remains there says a lot about the management of the hotel. Will the first hotel associate to pass through the area be trained well enough to realize that s/he should be on the look-out for such trash and discard it? If so, will s/he be motivated to do so if nobody is watching? The answers to both of the questions are largely dependent upon how well the hotel is managed and the culture that is fostered by management.

Further, it is also prudent to note that a number of surprise tactics can be creatively deployed as guests move through the public areas—particularly if children are in the group. This chapter, therefore, presents some such surprise tactics.

Technique #86

Display High Quality Outdoor Furniture

All outdoor furniture should be of high quality (even at limited service and economy properties). Viewing outdoor furniture subconsciously sets the tone for what the guest will receive once inside.

☐   We already practice this technique

☐   This technique would not be suitable for our operation

☐   We practiced this in the past and need to jumpstart

☐   We should implement this technique

Assigned to: _____

Projected Date of Implementation: _____

Technique #87

Keep Elevator Flooring Clean

Due to the use of rolling suitcases, one of the biggest problem areas with regard to public space cleanliness is the elevator floor. Staff should be trained to check and clean the flooring in the elevators several times per shift. The cleanliness of the elevator is a factor in initial perception formation and also influences guests' perceptions throughout their stay.

☐ We already practice this technique

☐ This technique would not be suitable for our operation

☐ We practiced this in the past and need to jumpstart

☐ We should implement this technique

Assigned to: _____

Projected Date of Implementation: _____

Technique #88

Offer Branded Rubber Duckies

When a family with a small child or baby passes a housekeeping cart in a corridor as they are returning to their guestroom, the housekeeper should offer the family a rubber duckie that is branded with the hotel's name/logo.

☐   We already practice this technique

☐   This technique would not be suitable for our operation

☐   We practiced this in the past and need to jumpstart

☐   We should implement this technique

Assigned to: _____

Projected Date of Implementation: _____

Technique #89

Create a Photo Zone

Photo Zone—With Selfies being the "in thing", create a backdrop, banner, or something unique to the hotel (including your logo or hotel name) where guests can take pictures of themselves or, if they want a photo with a camera, an employee can easily take a picture of the guests. Encourage guests to share it on social media or a blog. This is another way for guests to remember their experience in a positive way.

☐   We already practice this technique

☐   This technique would not be suitable for our operation

☐   We practiced this in the past and need to jumpstart

☐   We should implement this technique

Assigned to: _____

Projected Date of Implementation: _____

Technique #90

Routinely Eliminate Scuff Marks

At least two times per week, a member(s) of the engineering team should inspect all public corridors and remove scuff marks from walls with cleaning products such as Magic Erasers. This task should be part of the engineering team's preventative maintenance schedule.

❏   We already practice this technique

❏   This technique would not be suitable for our operation

❏   We practiced this in the past and need to jumpstart

❏   We should implement this technique

Assigned to: _____

Projected Date of Implementation: _____

Technique #91

Play Music in the Lobby

Music that matches the brand personality of the hotel should always be played in the lobby. Employees should understand the value of the music in reinforcing brand personality.

☐   We already practice this technique

☐   This technique would not be suitable for our operation

☐   We practiced this in the past and need to jumpstart

☐   We should implement this technique

Assigned to: _____

Projected Date of Implementation: _____

Technique #92

Scent the Lobby

The hotel's lobby should be scented year around with the same fragrance. Repeat guests will recall the scent when they return. This strategy can be achieved through plug-in aromatherapy products or by burning scented candles.

☐   We already practice this technique

☐   This technique would not be suitable for our operation

☐   We practiced this in the past and need to jumpstart

☐   We should implement this technique

Assigned to: _____

Projected Date of Implementation: _____

Technique #93

Afford Adequate Attention to Restroom Cleanliness

The public restroom cannot take a "rest" from service. The cleanliness and messiness of a restroom set the tone for other facets of a guest's experience. If a guest sees a dirty restroom, automatically s/he will have a negative impression of the hotel.

☐ We already practice this technique

☐ This technique would not be suitable for our operation

☐ We practiced this in the past and need to jumpstart

☐ We should implement this technique

Assigned to: _____

Projected Date of Implementation: _____

Technique #94

Use Bright Lighting in the Restroom

The hotel's public restrooms should have very bright fluorescent lighting. Such brightness helps the restroom appear clean.

☐ We already practice this technique

☐ This technique would not be suitable for our operation

☐ We practiced this in the past and need to jumpstart

☐ We should implement this technique

Assigned to: _____

Projected Date of Implementation: _____

Technique #95

Give Back-of-the-House Tours

When a potential catering and conference client arrives for a site visit, show him/her the back-of-the-house areas first. Including the back-of-the-house demonstrates that the hotel pays enough attention to detail to keep those areas neat and orderly similar to the front-of-the-house. This effort also aids in making the potential client feel as if s/he is getting to know the team.

☐ We already practice this technique

☐ This technique would not be suitable for our operation

☐ We practiced this in the past and need to jumpstart

☐ We should implement this technique

Assigned to: _____

Projected Date of Implementation: _____

Technique #96

Provide Employees with Business Cards

Have business cards with all the pertinent hotel information. Leave space on the card for an employee to be able to handwrite his/her name and position. Should a guest need hotel information, the employee can hand them out. This effort serves as a personalized service and the guest will know who to ask for if they need anything. This gesture comes in handy on many occasions and is fast and personalized as well.

❑ We already practice this technique

❑ This technique would not be suitable for our operation

❑ We practiced this in the past and need to jumpstart

❑ We should implement this technique

Assigned to: _____

Projected Date of Implementation: _____

Technique #97

Offer Branded Gloves

If a guest is exiting the hotel in the winter time without gloves, offer a complimentary pair of gloves branded with the hotel's logo.

☐   We already practice this technique

☐   This technique would not be suitable for our operation

☐   We practiced this in the past and need to jumpstart

☐   We should implement this technique

Assigned to: _____

Projected Date of Implementation: _____

Technique #98

Display a Looking Glass

If a window in one of the hotel's public spaces has a nice view, then affix a looking glass on a string to the wall next to the window.

❑   We already practice this technique

❑   This technique would not be suitable for our operation

❑   We practiced this in the past and need to jumpstart

❑   We should implement this technique

Assigned to: _____

Projected Date of Implementation: _____

Technique #99

Screen the Outdoor Break Area from Guest View

The hotel needs to have an outdoor break area for associates that are 100 percent screened from guest view. Such screening can be achieved with landscaping and/or decorative fencing. When a guest sees hotel associates on break smoking cigarettes, this is one of the biggest 'experience breaking' problems in the industry and is also one of the most common.

☐ We already practice this technique

☐ This technique would not be suitable for our operation

☐ We practiced this in the past and need to jumpstart

☐ We should implement this technique

Assigned to: _____

Projected Date of Implementation: _____

Technique #100

Offer Wagon Rides for Small Children

The hotel should have wagons in the lobby that are customized with a seat and side paneling so that families can give their children safe rides to their guestrooms. Customized wagons can also be available for pet transportation to the guestroom.

☐ We already practice this technique

☐ This technique would not be suitable for our operation

☐ We practiced this in the past and need to jumpstart

☐ We should implement this technique

Assigned to: _____

Projected Date of Implementation: _____

Technique #101

Have a Child-Sized Luggage Cart Available

Just as some grocery stores have child-sized grocery carts, a hotel can have a child-sized luggage cart. The child can help co-create the lodging experience by placing his/her suitcase on the small cart and pushing it to/from the guestroom at check-in/out.

☐ We already practice this technique

☐ This technique would not be suitable for our operation

☐ We practiced this in the past and need to jumpstart

☐ We should implement this technique

Assigned to: _____

Projected Date of Implementation: _____

Technique #102

Escort Guests to Local Attractions

If a guest(s) stops at the front desk or concierge desk and asks for walking directions to a nearby attraction, if an associate is available to do so, then the hotel can offer to escort the guest(s) to the attraction.

☐ We already practice this technique

☐ This technique would not be suitable for our operation

☐ We practiced this in the past and need to jumpstart

☐ We should implement this technique

Assigned to: _____

Projected Date of Implementation: _____

Technique #103

Make Bicycles Available

If the hotel is located in a bicycle-friendly area, then have some bicycles and helmets available to the guests at no charge. Guests can sign a liability waiver form and borrow the bicycles when desired.

☐ We already practice this technique

☐ This technique would not be suitable for our operation

☐ We practiced this in the past and need to jumpstart

☐ We should implement this technique

Assigned to: _____

Projected Date of Implementation: _____

Technique #104

Denote Empty Parking Spaces

· ·

When the hotel's parking lot or garage is near maximum capacity, helium balloons should be placed in the remaining parking spots. Viewing the balloons from a distance will allow guests the opportunity to find the open spots without wasting time or fuel.

☐   We already practice this technique

☐   This technique would not be suitable for our operation

☐   We practiced this in the past and need to jumpstart

☐   We should implement this technique

Assigned to: _____

Projected Date of Implementation: _____

Technique #105

Encourage Clutter-Free Storage Areas

Any areas that are visible to the guests when a door is open (e.g., service area, behind the front desk, office, storage room, etc.) should be free of clutter and anything that can be construed as unsanitary.

☐ We already practice this technique

☐ This technique would not be suitable for our operation

☐ We practiced this in the past and need to jumpstart

☐ We should implement this technique

Assigned to: _____

Projected Date of Implementation: _____

Technique #106

Conduct Signage Audits

At least once per year, a 3rd party who has never been inside the hotel before should be asked to do an internal and external signage audit to confirm that signs are accurate and are not confusing (particularly directional signs). The signage audit could be traded for a room night.

☐ We already practice this technique

☐ This technique would not be suitable for our operation

☐ We practiced this in the past and need to jumpstart

☐ We should implement this technique

Assigned to: _____

Projected Date of Implementation: _____

Technique #107

Print Hometowns on Nametags

All associates should have their hometowns printed on their nametags because this information helps facilitate conversation with guests.

☐   We already practice this technique

☐   This technique would not be suitable for our operation

☐   We practiced this in the past and need to jumpstart

☐   We should implement this technique

Assigned to: _____

Projected Date of Implementation: _____

Technique #108

Display Photos of Famous Locals

Display pictures of famous people from the local or surrounding area in the hotel's public spaces—doing so helps connect the guest to the hotel.

☐ We already practice this technique

☐ This technique would not be suitable for our operation

☐ We practiced this in the past and need to jumpstart

☐ We should implement this technique

Assigned to: _____

Projected Date of Implementation: _____

Technique #109

Offer Swimming-Related Amenities in Pool Area

If the hotel has a swimming pool, guests love the extras of a pool experience, especially in very hot weather. These items can be misters, cold washcloths, ice water, etc.

☐ We already practice this technique

☐ This technique would not be suitable for our operation

☐ We practiced this in the past and need to jumpstart

☐ We should implement this technique

Assigned to: _____

Projected Date of Implementation: _____

Technique #110

Offer to Augment Diving Toys with Gold or Silver Coins

If the hotel has a swimming pool, if children are seen diving for coins, they should be given gold or silver coins inscribed with the hotel name/logo to use instead. They can keep these as souvenirs.

☐   We already practice this technique

☐   This technique would not be suitable for our operation

☐   We practiced this in the past and need to jumpstart

☐   We should implement this technique

Assigned to: _____

Projected Date of Implementation: _____

Technique #111

Keep a Well-Stocked Bookcase

The hotel should have a bookcase in a public area from which guests can borrow books (including children's books) to read or games to play during their stay. Some books should be about the local area.

☐ We already practice this technique

☐ This technique would not be suitable for our operation

☐ We practiced this in the past and need to jumpstart

☐ We should implement this technique

Assigned to: _____

Projected Date of Implementation: _____

CHAPTER 7

The Food and Beverage Experience

There is a certain stigma associated with hotel food and beverage. However unpleasant to read, the stigma is the blunt reality. Sure, most hotel industry veterans can likely name a handful of hotel restaurant success stories, but hotel restaurants that operate in the red and are rationalized by management as a guest amenity are far more common than the successful ones.

"One cannot think well, love well, sleep well, if one has not dined well"

—*Virginia Woolf*

In every weakness, there is opportunity: low guest expectations can actually serve as opportunities for hoteliers. The most common conceptualization of how consumers' satisfaction judgments are formulated is termed the expectancy disconfirmation paradigm (EDP). According to EDP, if an individual's actual experience falls short of expectations then s/he is left dissatisfied, but if an individual's actual experience exceeds expectations then s/he is left satisfied [12]. In line with EDP logic, if guests possess low expectations, but circumstances mandate a consumption experience, such a scenario presents an opportunity to impress.

An ideal scenario, for example, is breakfast—the busiest meal period in hotels. Whether breakfast is included in the price of the sleeping room or not, the meal period has a high capture rate due to the convenience of consuming the meal in the hotel. Research indicates that the quality of the breakfast experience plays a key role in determining a guest's overall satisfaction with his/her stay. That is, the breakfast experience is a key driver of guest satisfaction [13]. The quality of the breakfast meal experience, with regard to both food and service, must be skillfully managed in a hotel. This chapter, therefore, offers some techniques that can be applied to this area.

Banquet experiences also present opportunities for hotels with meeting facilities to shine. Not only the financial margins are in the favor of the hotel for such business, but also the potential to shine is abundant in such scenarios because the organizers of such functions have high levels of psychological involvement—you as a hotelier have their full attention. High levels of psychological involvement are not only a consequence of the financial outlay (financial risk) that a group function entails, but are also a result of the social risk—whether a wedding reception, a business meeting, or a family reunion the organizer who selected the hotel venue would be embarrassed if the hotel performs poorly. This psychological involvement of the client driven by financial and social risk is a key opportunity for the hotel and should be capitalized on.

Technique #112

Host Menu Tastings for Staff

All frontline staff in the hotel should have knowledge of the restaurant menu items. This knowledge is needed in order for them to feel confident in making recommendations and upselling. In this effort, staff should periodically be invited to taste items.

☐   We already practice this technique

☐   This technique would not be suitable for our operation

☐   We practiced this in the past and need to jumpstart

☐   We should implement this technique

Assigned to: _____

Projected Date of Implementation: _____

Technique #113

Hang a Mirror in the Service Area

Hang a full-length mirror in the expo area of the kitchen so that servers can check their appearance throughout their shift.

☐ We already practice this technique

☐ This technique would not be suitable for our operation

☐ We practiced this in the past and need to jumpstart

☐ We should implement this technique

Assigned to: _____

Projected Date of Implementation: _____

Technique #114

Use Strong Language When Checking on Tables

Servers should never ask diners 'Is everything OK?' Being 'OK' is a low standard and does not foster or communicate a culture of excellence. Instead servers should ask more situation-specific question such as 'How is your omelet?' If a situation-specific question cannot be formulated, the server should ask 'How is everything?'

☐ We already practice this technique

☐ This technique would not be suitable for our operation

☐ We practiced this in the past and need to jumpstart

☐ We should implement this technique

Assigned to: _____

Projected Date of Implementation: _____

Technique #115

Identify Congestion Points in the Breakfast Buffet

Due to the sheer number of guests that dine in the hotel for breakfast, it is the most important meal period for the hotel to get right. In a buffet setting, management should routinely observe where guest congestion is prone to occur during the buffet experience. Often, congestion points can be alleviated with better signage, altered buffet layout, and by repositioning certain items.

☐ We already practice this technique

☐ This technique would not be suitable for our operation

☐ We practiced this in the past and need to jumpstart

☐ We should implement this technique

Assigned to: _____

Projected Date of Implementation: _____

Technique #116

Improve Efficiency at the Made-to-Order Egg Station

Often, the congestion point in the hotel breakfast experience is the made-to-order egg station. Typically, this congestion occurs because the chef working the station is not properly trained. The chef should be trained to begin heating the saute pans as s/he sees guests approaching the station. In addition, toppings should be finely diced so that they can saute faster. When no guests are in view of the station, s/he can practice his/her flipping speed and accuracy by using a slice of bread in the pans. S/he should also be well stocked with both egg whites and egg substitutes because the demand for these items is increasing as baby boomers age. A well-trained chef should be able to prepare three orders simultaneously at the station (always keep a fire extinguisher at the station).

- ☐ We already practice this technique
- ☐ This technique would not be suitable for our operation
- ☐ We practiced this in the past and need to jumpstart
- ☐ We should implement this technique

Assigned to: _____

Projected Date of Implementation: _____

Technique #117

Improve Efficiency at the Belgian Waffle Station

A common congestion point in the breakfast buffet area is the Belgian waffle station. Substituting the typical waffle irons with irons that can produce four miniature waffles simultaneously should alleviate some/most of the congestion. Rather than taking a full-sized Belgian waffle (which is too large for most guests who also want to try other foods), the guest can instead take two mini-waffles.

☐ We already practice this technique

☐ This technique would not be suitable for our operation

☐ We practiced this in the past and need to jumpstart

☐ We should implement this technique

Assigned to: _____

Projected Date of Implementation: _____

Technique #118

Have a To-Go Breakfast Option Available

If a guest requests an early wake-up call or asks to get a cab at a time before the restaurant opens, offer a bagged breakfast that can be made up the night before. Items in the to-go breakfast bag might include a muffin, breakfast bar, apple, bottled water etc. This to-go breakfast does not have to be complimentary; this gesture of goodwill goes a long way.

☐ We already practice this technique

☐ This technique would not be suitable for our operation

☐ We practiced this in the past and need to jumpstart

☐ We should implement this technique

Assigned to: _____

Projected Date of Implementation: _____

Technique #119

Offer Customizable Chef Hats to Children

Rather than standard coloring sheets, the restaurant should instead have paper chef hats for small children that can be colored and decorated.

☐ We already practice this technique

☐ This technique would not be suitable for our operation

☐ We practiced this in the past and need to jumpstart

☐ We should implement this technique

Assigned to: _____

Projected Date of Implementation: _____

Technique #120

Offer Origami Kits to Children

Rather than standard coloring sheets, the restaurant should instead have origami kits for elementary-aged children.

☐ We already practice this technique

☐ This technique would not be suitable for our operation

☐ We practiced this in the past and need to jumpstart

☐ We should implement this technique

Assigned to: _____

Projected Date of Implementation: _____

Technique #121

Let Small Children Play with Dough

If the restaurant uses bread, pastry, or pizza dough in any recipes, small children should be offered a small piece of dough on a paper plate that they can play with while waiting for meals.

☐ We already practice this technique

☐ This technique would not be suitable for our operation

☐ We practiced this in the past and need to jumpstart

☐ We should implement this technique

Assigned to: _____

Projected Date of Implementation: _____

Technique #122

Inscribe Surprise Messages Inside Coffee Cups

The inside of some of the restaurant's coffee cups can be randomly inscribed with messages such as "We hope that you are enjoying your stay!"

☐ We already practice this technique

☐ This technique would not be suitable for our operation

☐ We practiced this in the past and need to jumpstart

☐ We should implement this technique

Assigned to: _____

Projected Date of Implementation: _____

Technique #123

Use Strong Language When Greeting Restaurant Guests

Restaurant greeters should never use the word "JUST" when verifying the number of guests in a dining party. If there are "just" 1 or 2 people, the word diminishes the worth of the diners who are present. Welcome all equally.

☐ We already practice this technique

☐ This technique would not be suitable for our operation

☐ We practiced this in the past and need to jumpstart

☐ We should implement this technique

Assigned to: _____

Projected Date of Implementation: _____

Technique #124

Extend VIP Invitations to Valued Guests

If a local is dining in the restaurant, invite him/her to be a VIP at an upcoming menu tasting or wine tasting.

☐ We already practice this technique

☐ This technique would not be suitable for our operation

☐ We practiced this in the past and need to jumpstart

☐ We should implement this technique

Assigned to: _____

Projected Date of Implementation: _____

Technique #125

Play Peek-A-Boo

Servers should be trained that one tactic that can be used to bring a smile to a baby's face is a quick game of peek-a-boo while visiting the table.

☐   We already practice this technique

☐   This technique would not be suitable for our operation

☐   We practiced this in the past and need to jumpstart

☐   We should implement this technique

Assigned to: _____

Projected Date of Implementation: _____

Technique #126

Promote Table Bussing Efficiency

During busy breakfast periods, often tables cannot be turned because there is a lag in bussing, cleaning, and resetting them. Bussers should be staffed heavily, bussers should be compensated well (maybe through a tip pool), associates from other departments should be cross-trained as bussers, and ample supplies should be on hand for table reset. Often, when associates from other departments aid in bussing and resetting, they are so poorly cross-trained that their help is inefficient and can even get in the way. Furthermore, the breakfast restaurant supervisor or manager should have a laminated checklist of all table resetting supplies and should check the par levels of all of these items before a shift begins.

❑ We already practice this technique

❑ This technique would not be suitable for our operation

❑ We practiced this in the past and need to jumpstart

❑ We should implement this technique

Assigned to: _____

Projected Date of Implementation: _____

Technique #127

Have a Children's Treasure Chest Available

Treat the child guest with a treasure chest of toys. The hotel does not have to spend a lot of money on the toys; they can be from the dollar store or similar. Let the child pick a toy from the chest. The child will be happy and excited and the adult guest will be very appreciative. This is an excellent and inexpensive way to exhibit outstanding guest service at the commencement of a dining experience.

☐   We already practice this technique

☐   This technique would not be suitable for our operation

☐   We practiced this in the past and need to jumpstart

☐   We should implement this technique

Assigned to: _____

Projected Date of Implementation: _____

- ☐ We already practice this technique
- ☐ This technique would not be suitable for our operation
- ☐ We practiced this in the past and need to jumpstart
- ☐ We should implement this technique

Assigned to: _____

Projected Date of Implementation: _____

Technique #128

Use Language That Encourages Dessert Upselling

"Are you too full for dessert?" When a server asks this question it assumes that the guest does not want dessert and s/he wants to turn your table; not a positive ending to a dinner. Instead, servers should be taught to upsell desserts with lines such as "We have fabulous desserts;" "I hope you left room for one;" and "Let me tell you about them."

☐ We already practice this technique

☐ This technique would not be suitable for our operation

☐ We practiced this in the past and need to jumpstart

☐ We should implement this technique

Assigned to: _____

Projected Date of Implementation: _____

CHAPTER 8

The Check-Out Experience

G uests are not obligated to check-out at the front desk: it is perfectly acceptable to leave the key cards on the nightstand and continue with one's travel itinerary. Therefore, if a guest does choose to engage in a face-to-face encounter at check-out, the hotel should capitalize on the opportunity to further solidify the relationship.

"Leverage is the strength that you have: that no one else can be you"

—Todd Wheatland

In order to be effective ambassadors and salespeople of the hotel, all associates need to genuinely believe that the hotel provides experiences that are meaningful and of value to the guests. The hotel business is competitive: in most markets, guests have numerous lodging options. Consequently, front desk associates who are checking out guests should have a level of confidence in his/her coworkers that the experience that was provided was a valuable one that could not have been readily delivered by a competitor.

Such confidence should be drawn upon in the check-out conversation to achieve three objectives: (i) communicate gratitude to the guest for choosing the property; (ii) establish a level of rapport in which the guest feels comfortable providing meaningful feedback regarding the stay; and (iii) further solidify the relationship so that the guest will remain loyal to the property and/or brand.

Rapport is critical to gaining valuable feedback about the concluding stay. To illustrate the importance of rapport in generating meaningful feedback, we can use an actual example from the recreation sector. There is a network of very well-managed public parks that have a 98 percent user return intent and also have a 98 percent positive word-of-mouth intent—year after year. On the same surveys from which these statistics derive, about 1 out of 6 visitors offers a handwritten suggestion for improvement in the survey's comment section [14]. This example illustrates that if a patron feels a strong connection with a provider then s/he is more likely to offer genuine and useful feedback.

It is also important to note in this chapter, that associates can contribute to a meaningful check-out—even if they do not work at the front desk. All associates in the hotel, from housekeepers to restaurant servers, should realize that when a guest is rolling a suitcase in the AM hours then s/he is checking out. Thus, it becomes the responsibility of all associates to thank the guest for his/her business and invite him/her to return.

Although somewhat of a cliché: last impressions can make a lasting impression. It is the final part of an interaction that is most likely to be salient in the mind of the consumer for the longest period of time [15]. Because of the level of attention that our minds assign to the concluding portions of transactions, the hotel check-out provides an opportunity to impress.

Technique #129

Encourage Fond Farewells from Housekeepers

All housekeepers should thank guests for their business and invite them to return when they see guests exiting down guestroom corridors. If a guest is rolling luggage down a corridor in the AM hours, it is evident that s/he is checking out.

☐ We already practice this technique

☐ This technique would not be suitable for our operation

☐ We practiced this in the past and need to jumpstart

☐ We should implement this technique

Assigned to: _____

Projected Date of Implementation: _____

Technique #130

Clean Guests' Windshields

Each morning, the hotel should randomly select approximately 10 vehicles of guests who are checking out and clean their windshields. A note can be placed on the vehicle so that the departing guest will notice that the windshield has been cleaned.

☐ We already practice this technique

☐ This technique would not be suitable for our operation

☐ We practiced this in the past and need to jumpstart

☐ We should implement this technique

Assigned to: _____

Projected Date of Implementation: _____

Technique #131

Offer Auto Snow/Ice Removal Tools

· ·

In cold climates, have snow/ice removal tools handy. When a guest checks out, these items will be useful for the guest's vehicle. For added service, a staff member can clean the vehicle quickly for the guest.

☐ We already practice this technique

☐ This technique would not be suitable for our operation

☐ We practiced this in the past and need to jumpstart

☐ We should implement this technique

Assigned to: _____

Projected Date of Implementation: _____

Technique #132

Offer Room Keys to Children as Souvenirs

When a guest is checking out with small children, the room key cards should be offered to the children as souvenirs. Children can even be offered craft kits so that they can decorate the key cards with jewels, stickers, or pipe cleaners while traveling home.

☐ We already practice this technique

☐ This technique would not be suitable for our operation

☐ We practiced this in the past and need to jumpstart

☐ We should implement this technique

Assigned to: _____

Projected Date of Implementation: _____

Technique #133

Offer Children Coins Inscribed with the Hotel's Logo

When a family with children is checking out, the children can be given gold or silver coins that are inscribed with the hotel name and logo.

☐ We already practice this technique

☐ This technique would not be suitable for our operation

☐ We practiced this in the past and need to jumpstart

☐ We should implement this technique

Assigned to: _____

Projected Date of Implementation: _____

Technique #134

Let Guests Take $1 Bills

The front office manager should fill a glass fish bowl with $1 bills. One morning per week, the bowl can be placed on the front desk with a sign that reads: "If you are checking out, please take a few of these for the road." The actual sight of currency is actually much more powerful than simply discounting a guest's folio.

☐   We already practice this technique

☐   This technique would not be suitable for our operation

☐   We practiced this in the past and need to jumpstart

☐   We should implement this technique

Assigned to: _____

Projected Date of Implementation: _____

Technique #135

Inform Guests of Potential Bank-Related Issues Associated with the Use of Debit Cards

Debit Cards can be a challenge when using them at a hotel. Any guests using a debit card should be made aware of how the bank "holds" the money. It can be helpful to have the desk clerk explain this to the guest beforehand. No matter what experience the guest had at the hotel, if s/he has issues related to finances, such issues can ruin an otherwise positive experience.

❏ We already practice this technique

❏ This technique would not be suitable for our operation

❏ We practiced this in the past and need to jumpstart

❏ We should implement this technique

Assigned to: _____

Projected Date of Implementation: _____

Technique #136

Offer to Store Items for Frequent Guests

If you have a guest that stays weekly, offer to store some of his/her items so that s/he do not have to take them home each week. Even if s/he does not want to utilize this service, the offer will likely mean a lot.

☐   We already practice this technique

☐   This technique would not be suitable for our operation

☐   We practiced this in the past and need to jumpstart

☐   We should implement this technique

Assigned to: _____

Projected Date of Implementation: _____

Technique #137

Send a Gift Home to a Child

If a guest is traveling alone on business, but the property management system indicates that s/he has stayed in the past with a child then consider asking the guest if s/he would like a small gift to take home to the child.

☐ We already practice this technique

☐ This technique would not be suitable for our operation

☐ We practiced this in the past and need to jumpstart

☐ We should implement this technique

Assigned to: _____

Projected Date of Implementation: _____

Technique #138

Give Some Fresh Vegetables or Herbs

If the hotel has a garden and a vegetable or fruit is ripe, offer the guest at check-out 1–2 pieces to take home (similar to how friends and family share items from their home gardens). Or, have a herb garden growing inside one or more lobby windows and ask the guest if s/he would like to cut some herbs to take home.

☐ We already practice this technique

☐ This technique would not be suitable for our operation

☐ We practiced this in the past and need to jumpstart

☐ We should implement this technique

Assigned to: _____

Projected Date of Implementation: _____

1	2	3	4	5	6	7	8	9	10
11	12	13	14	15	16	17	18	19	20
21	22	23	24	25	26	27	28	29	30
31	32	33	34	35	36	37	38	39	40
41	42	43	44	45	46	47	48	49	50
51	52	53	54	55	56	57	58	59	60
61	62	63	64	65	66	67	68	69	70
71	72	73	74	75	76	77	78	79	80
81	82	83	84	85	86	87	88	89	90
91	92	93	94	95	96	97	98	99	100
101	102	103	104	105	106	107	108	109	110
111	112	113	114	115	116	117	118	119	120
121	122	123	124	125	126	127	128	129	130
131	132	133	134	135	136	137	138	**139**	**140**
141	**142**	**143**	**144**	**145**	**146**	**147**	**148**	**149**	**150**
151	**152**	**153**	**154**	**155**	**156**	**157**	**158**	**159**	**160**
161	**162**	**163**	**164**	**165**	**166**	167	168	169	170
171	172	173	174	175	176	177	178	179	180
181	182	183	184	185	186	187	188	189	

Section III

• • • • • • • • • • • • • •

Managing the Critical Drivers of Service Scores

PREVIEW

Research indicates that a few key areas have sizable impacts on guest sentiment. One of these key areas is service failure recovery—when something goes wrong, the hotel has the guest's full attention. The second critical area is forecasting/contingency plans—the hotel must accurately forecast business levels and have plans in place to deliver top-rate service when actual business levels exceed forecasted levels. The third key area is perceived waiting times—once in the hotel, guests do not like waiting to participate in the various stages of experience consumption.

CHAPTER **9**

Service Failure Recovery

In the hotel business, due to the high human component and the many moving parts, things are bound to go wrong from time to time. For example, even a top-rate engineering team cannot prevent power outages or water supply problems. Neverthe-less, while a certain portion of problems and failures are inevitable in the hotel sector, such problems and failures do not necessarily need to yield dissatisfied guests. In fact, it is often possible to receive higher satisfaction ratings from a guest after a failure than if the situation had never occurred.

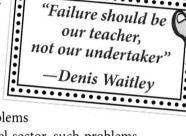

"Failure should be our teacher, not our undertaker"

—Denis Waitley

The recovery paradox refers to the notion that a service failure might offer an opportunity to receive higher satisfaction ratings from guests than if the scenario had never occurred—but only if you deliver an excellent failure recovery [16]. Stated differently, if you offer a first-rate recovery, then your guests might feel a stronger bond with you than they did before the failure. Because guests often understand that some problems and failures are inevitable, the fact that you went the extra-mile to remedy the problem signals your integrity. Guests become very observant of your actions after a service failure because the situation has caused the transaction to deviate from their "mental script" of what they anticipated [17]. Consequently, this heightened guest attention opens a window for you to impress.

Evidently a number of conditions must be in place in order to catapult guest satisfaction after a failure. First, the failure recovery that you and your staff demonstrate must be well-orchestrated. Second, it is unlikely that a recovery paradox will occur if it is the guest's second failure in your hotel [18]. Third, if the guest perceives the likelihood of reoccurrence as high than s/he will not view the situation favorably [19]. Fourth, if the failure is too severe it is unlikely that an excellent recovery can spawn paradoxical increases in satisfaction [20].

It is important to note that handling a failure properly can trigger a recovery paradox, but conversely, not handling the failure properly can result in a double deviation effect. Double deviation is the term used to describe a situation in which your hotel is made aware of a problem, but the resolution offered by your staff is so poor that, in the eyes of the guest, the resolution is viewed as a second failure [21]. As one might imagine, double deviations can be very detrimental to the health of your property. This chapter, therefore, offers a number of techniques related to high-performance failure recovery. Some techniques focus specifically upon situations in which the failure was out of the control of the hotel because offering guests relief in such situations is a particularly effective means of spawning recovery paradoxes.

Technique #139

Ask About Travel Experiences

Offering redress for problems not caused by the hotel can be a key driver of guest satisfaction. For example, if a guest mentions travel-related problems experienced before arrival, the hotel should offer an amenity or upgrade as an expression of empathy and comfort. Front desk associates should be encouraged to ask guests how their trips were because doing so increases the probability of finding out about travel-related frustrations.

- ☐ We already practice this technique
- ☐ This technique would not be suitable for our operation
- ☐ We practiced this in the past and need to jumpstart
- ☐ We should implement this technique

Assigned to: _____

Projected Date of Implementation: _____

Technique #140

Thank Guests for Complaining

All associates should be trained to thank guests when they voice valid complaints. Such a thank you encourage guests to communicate problems directly with the provider as opposed to posting complaints on social media forums. Thanking the guest for voicing the complaint also signals that the problem is less likely reoccur in the future.

☐ We already practice this technique

☐ This technique would not be suitable for our operation

☐ We practiced this in the past and need to jumpstart

☐ We should implement this technique

Assigned to: _____

Projected Date of Implementation: _____

Technique #141

Ask What Would Fix the Problem

If a guest voices a valid complaint, after listening, empathizing, thanking the guest, and apologizing, the hotel associate should ask the guest what the hotel can do to fix the problem. Most guests will ask for very little which presents the opportunity to deliver more than what was asked—spawning guest delight.

☐ We already practice this technique

☐ This technique would not be suitable for our operation

☐ We practiced this in the past and need to jumpstart

☐ We should implement this technique

Assigned to: _____

Projected Date of Implementation: _____

Technique #142

Organize Recharging Cords

Recharging cords for mobile electronics are perhaps the most commonly left items in the rooms; thus, most hotels have excess in lost and found since many guests never call for them. Therefore, the hotel should have a selection already identified by phone/computer type. When a guest asks where to buy one, or if they ask to borrow one from the hotel, they will be readily available for them to use with no hassle.

☐ We already practice this technique

☐ This technique would not be suitable for our operation

☐ We practiced this in the past and need to jumpstart

☐ We should implement this technique

Assigned to: _____

Projected Date of Implementation: _____

Technique #143

Be Ready for Clean-Up

•••

The front desk agent should always have immediate access to both cloth towels and paper towels and should be on the look-out for guests in need of them. They can be offered if a guest comes in from the rain, if an infant spits up, etc.

❑ We already practice this technique

❑ This technique would not be suitable for our operation

❑ We practiced this in the past and need to jumpstart

❑ We should implement this technique

Assigned to: _____

Projected Date of Implementation: _____

Technique #144

Have Shower Chairs and Bath Mats Readily Available

While all hotels have handicap rooms, at times, an elderly person or a person with an ailment may want "more protection" while in the shower. A shower chair and rubber bath mats are good to have on hand.

☐ We already practice this technique

☐ This technique would not be suitable for our operation

☐ We practiced this in the past and need to jumpstart

☐ We should implement this technique

Assigned to: _____

Projected Date of Implementation: _____

Technique #145

Offer Hot Chocolate During Inclement Weather

Whether driving or flying, guests' stress levels increase significantly when they must attempt to travel in snow or ice. Hot chocolate should be available in the lobby in such circumstances.

☐ We already practice this technique

☐ This technique would not be suitable for our operation

☐ We practiced this in the past and need to jumpstart

☐ We should implement this technique

Assigned to: _____

Projected Date of Implementation: _____

Technique #146

Let Guests Keep Umbrellas

The hotel should have an abundance of umbrellas at the front desk for guests to use when needed. If a guest says s/he will drive the car around and return it later, let them keep the umbrella (they can be purchased inexpensively at a dollar store).

☐ We already practice this technique

☐ This technique would not be suitable for our operation

☐ We practiced this in the past and need to jumpstart

☐ We should implement this technique

Assigned to: _____

Projected Date of Implementation: _____

Technique #147

Organize Unclaimed Items Suitable for Borrowing

Many times clothing, belts, etc. are left in lost and found. If the items remain unclaimed, they can be used for guests to borrow if forgotten to pack. A closet, or part of a closet, can be dedicated to these items.

☐   We already practice this technique

☐   This technique would not be suitable for our operation

☐   We practiced this in the past and need to jumpstart

☐   We should implement this technique

Assigned to: _____

Projected Date of Implementation: _____

Technique #148

Be Informed About Guest Assistance Information

Guests continue to have more special needs as it relates to medical and dietary. Ensure that desk and restaurant staffs have the basic knowledge to assist the guests with these concerns. The key is where to direct them so they can get the information they need, such as what restaurant serves the needed food; pharmacy information; dentist information; or medical emergency information. To have information ahead of time will help when the need arises so the situation can be dealt with immediately.

☐   We already practice this technique

☐   This technique would not be suitable for our operation

☐   We practiced this in the past and need to jumpstart

☐   We should implement this technique

Assigned to: _____

Projected Date of Implementation: _____

Technique #149

Have a List of Languages Spoken by Staff

Many hotel personnel speak multiple languages. Have a list of any employee that speaks different languages. When there is a guest who needs additional interpretation it will be helpful to know who the employees are that can help them. With foreign travel getting stronger, this is very valuable to the hotel.

☐ We already practice this technique

☐ This technique would not be suitable for our operation

☐ We practiced this in the past and need to jumpstart

☐ We should implement this technique

Assigned to: _____

Projected Date of Implementation: _____

Technique #150

Have a System for Handling Verbal Communication Barriers

If an associate does not speak English, then s/he should carry cards to give to the guest so when they ask a question, they can explain this and direct them to someone who can help immediately. The staff member can also have a pen and paper readily available to help facilitate communication; be sure there is a system in place for this sort of communication. To ignore the guest is a failure in guest service.

☐ We already practice this technique

☐ This technique would not be suitable for our operation

☐ We practiced this in the past and need to jumpstart

☐ We should implement this technique

Assigned to: _____

Projected Date of Implementation: _____

 *Technique #151*

Recognize Employees for Exceptional Service Failure Recovery Efforts

If an associate goes the extra-mile to solve a guest's problem, take a digital photo of the associate and write a few sentence narrative about what s/he did in the situation. Use the narrative and photo to make a small poster that can be hung in the employee break room.

☐ We already practice this technique

☐ This technique would not be suitable for our operation

☐ We practiced this in the past and need to jumpstart

☐ We should implement this technique

Assigned to: _____

Projected Date of Implementation: _____

CHAPTER 10

Forecasting and Contingency Plans

Consistently high-quality service in a hotel can only be achieved if departmental managers can accurately forecast business volumes in their respective areas. Because managers often possess a reasonably accurate occupancy estimate when departmental forecasts are crafted, it can be said that a sound departmental forecast hinges upon understanding the behaviors of various guest segments. More specifically, predicting the timing and levels of guest visitation and usage of departmental offerings entails understanding the guest in terms of his/her needs, wants, and preferences [22].

> "For most representatives, the choice between working on the forecast and getting a root canal would lead to a trip to the dentist."
>
> —Scott Edinger

Even the most seasoned hoteliers cannot accurately predict departmental business volumes in every situation. Who would have known that the *ABC Association of XYZ Professionals* staying in the hotel would have all convened at the lobby bar for drinks and appetizers? This gathering might have been particularly tricky to forecast because the group's contact with the hotel did not predict this impromptu gathering either. This gathering might have also been difficult to prognosticate because the group did not patronize the lobby bar in their previous stay at the hotel. Regardless of these circumstances, if these *XYZ Professionals* need wait an hour for a cheese quesadilla or 75 minutes for an order of chicken wings, you might imagine how guest satisfaction scores might look when they are collected and tabulated. The moral of this example is evident: even the best forecasters will get things wrong every now and then—estimation errors are inevitable. Therefore, well-orchestrated contingency plans must be seamlessly executed when actual business levels exceed forecasted levels.

This chapter offers a number of techniques that can be used to aid in forecasting as well as some measures that can be put in place as contingency strategies when actual business volumes exceed forecasted levels. Departmental managers should be trained to act like football coaches in that they read situations as they unfold and make adjustments on the fly with their teams to provide seamless service. Doing so is easier said than done: for instance, nearly all managers claim that their associates are cross-trained, but when scenarios unfold, many associates cross-trained perform so poorly that shifting to a secondary area often makes the situation slower and less efficient (e.g., how can a hotel front desk agent adequately work at the restaurant greeter stand if s/he does not know where the children's menus and crayons are kept?). In summary, the intended goals of offering the techniques in this chapter are to: (i) reduce the number of occurrences of inaccurate forecasts; and (ii) help ensure adequate guest service when inaccurate forecasting does occur.

Technique #152

Install a Doorbell Behind the Front Desk

Install a doorbell behind the front desk that the agent can ring when the desk gets busy unexpectedly. The bell can sound in a back-of-the-house area where one or more individuals are cross-trained to operate the property management system.

☐ We already practice this technique

☐ This technique would not be suitable for our operation

☐ We practiced this in the past and need to jumpstart

☐ We should implement this technique

Assigned to: _____

Projected Date of Implementation: _____

Technique #153

Install a Direct Telephone Line from the Front Desk to the Kitchen

If the front desk gets busy unexpectedly, there should be a direct telephone line that rings from the front desk to the kitchen so that food can be brought out immediately to guests waiting for front desk service. All front desk agents and cooks should be both trained and empowered to act swiftly in such a circumstance. Cookies would suffice in such a situation, but have become relatively commonplace at front desks; therefore, more creative items such as fudge might have a more powerful effect.

☐ We already practice this technique

☐ This technique would not be suitable for our operation

☐ We practiced this in the past and need to jumpstart

☐ We should implement this technique

Assigned to: _____

Projected Date of Implementation: _____

Technique #154

Telephone the Guest When His/Her Room is Ready for Check-In

• •

When a guest checks in early, but there is not a room ready, ask the guest if s/he would like to be called when there is one available. If so, make sure that s/he is called in a timely manner; this gesture goes a long way in terms of customer satisfaction.

☐ We already practice this technique

☐ This technique would not be suitable for our operation

☐ We practiced this in the past and need to jumpstart

☐ We should implement this technique

Assigned to: _____

Projected Date of Implementation: _____

Technique #155

Produce Laminated Room Inspection Checklists

All managers in the hotel should be provided with condensed laminated guestroom inspection checklists. The checklists should be small enough to carry in a pocket. When the housekeeping department is stressed, managers from other departments should be called to do room inspections.

☐ We already practice this technique

☐ This technique would not be suitable for our operation

☐ We practiced this in the past and need to jumpstart

☐ We should implement this technique

Assigned to: _____

Projected Date of Implementation: _____

Technique #156

Post Par-Levels for All Supplies

All departments should have posted par-levels for all supplies. The person who confirms the par-level for the given items should initial the posted par-level sheet. Often, service systems deteriorate because associates do not have the supplies that they need.

☐ We already practice this technique

☐ This technique would not be suitable for our operation

☐ We practiced this in the past and need to jumpstart

☐ We should implement this technique

Assigned to: _____

Projected Date of Implementation: _____

Technique #157

Analyze Why a Forecast Was Incorrect

If the forecast for a particular area of the hotel was inaccurate, and service quality suffered as a consequence, at the next management meeting a discussion should be held as to why the forecast was inaccurate. This practice is particularly germane to examining lunch and dinner capture rates in the restaurant outlet(s).

☐ We already practice this technique

☐ This technique would not be suitable for our operation

☐ We practiced this in the past and need to jumpstart

☐ We should implement this technique

Assigned to: _____

Projected Date of Implementation: _____

Perceived Waiting Times

Hotel guests do not like to wait for service; they don't want to wait to check-in; to be seated for breakfast; for their room to be cleaned; for the valet to bring the car, etc. Whether the stay is for business, leisure, or a combination, guests would rather enjoy consuming the various stages of the hospitality experience as opposed to waiting for them to begin. Therefore, waiting times have a direct impact on guest satisfaction scores.

> *A 5 minute wait can feel like either a 7 minute wait or a 3 minute wait.*

Due to the simultaneous production and consumption that occurs in our business, some guest waiting is inevitable in most areas of the hotel. Fortunately, research indicates that there are often discrepancies between actual and perceived waiting times. That is, a five-minute wait can feel like a seven-minute wait or a three-minute wait depending upon how it is managed by the hotel [23]. Using exiting research as an anchor, this chapter offers a series of techniques that can be used in hotels to make perceived waiting times feel shorter than actual waiting times.

Before some or all of the techniques in this chapter are implemented at your property, it is recommended that a simple exercise be used to illustrate to your staff the importance of managing perceived waiting times. In this exercise, you should gather your staff together in a quiet room and ask them to close their eyes and remain silent while their eyes are closed. Using a timer, you should ask them to open their eyes when 60 seconds have passed. Once their eyes are opened, ask them to write down an estimate regarding how long their eyes were closed. In this exercise, most (if not all) will estimate the time being longer than 60 seconds—most will likely write times between 90 seconds and two minutes. In this scenario, it should then be explained to the staff participants that the perceived waiting time felt longer than actual waiting time due to the lack of visual or auditory cues to mentally occupy them. This exercise is a means by which to demonstrate how easily a mismatch can occur between actual and perceived waiting lengths and the need to actively manage cues to reduce perceived waiting durations. It will follow that staff members will be more supportive of embracing and implementing the techniques in this chapter once this demonstration has occurred.

Technique #158

Put a Bell on the Front Desk

The front desk should have a bell for guests to ring. If a guest comes by and the desk clerk is in the back, the guest will not have to wait to get recognized or get service. CAUTION: The bell is not an excuse for desk agents to linger behind the scenes.

❑ We already practice this technique

❑ This technique would not be suitable for our operation

❑ We practiced this in the past and need to jumpstart

❑ We should implement this technique

Assigned to: _____

Projected Date of Implementation: _____

Technique #159

Hang Mirrors Outside Elevator Doors

Hang at least one mirror on each floor by the elevators. Perceived waiting time for the elevator is reduced when guests can look in mirrors.

☐   We already practice this technique

☐   This technique would not be suitable for our operation

☐   We practiced this in the past and need to jumpstart

☐   We should implement this technique

Assigned to: _____

Projected Date of Implementation: _____

Technique #160

Greet Guests While They Are Waiting to Check-In

Perceived waiting time is reduced when a process begins. Because part of the check-in process is being greeted, when the front desk gets busy unexpectedly, a hotel representative from another department can greet and talk with guests as they wait in line.

❑ We already practice this technique

❑ This technique would not be suitable for our operation

❑ We practiced this in the past and need to jumpstart

❑ We should implement this technique

Assigned to: _____

Projected Date of Implementation: _____

Technique #161

Tastefully Display Information Inside Elevators

The displaying of information inside guest elevators not only serves to reduce perceived waiting times but is also an outstanding opportunity for advertising your hotel and the area. Displaying appropriate and tasteful information can increase guest engagement.

☐ We already practice this technique

☐ This technique would not be suitable for our operation

☐ We practiced this in the past and need to jumpstart

☐ We should implement this technique

Assigned to: _____

Projected Date of Implementation: _____

Technique #162

Offer Food and Beverage at the Front Desk When Busy

Providing something small to eat or drink (e.g., cookie; infused water) at the front desk serves to reduce perceived waiting times of guests at the desk.

- ☐ We already practice this technique
- ☐ This technique would not be suitable for our operation
- ☐ We practiced this in the past and need to jumpstart
- ☐ We should implement this technique

Assigned to: _____

Projected Date of Implementation: _____

Technique #163

Create Strategic Alliances to Permit the Use of Hotel Key Cards at Local Attractions

The hotel should establish strategic alliances with local attractions by which the hotel's room key can be used to gain admittance to the attractions. Such relationships could reduce/eliminate the waiting that the guests would experience when purchasing tickets at the attractions.

☐ We already practice this technique

☐ This technique would not be suitable for our operation

☐ We practiced this in the past and need to jumpstart

☐ We should implement this technique

Assigned to: _____

Projected Date of Implementation: _____

Technique #164

Have Pre-Printed Directions Readily Available

Do guests repeatedly ask for directions for the same place like getting on the highway, the big office park, etc.? The front desk agents should have small pieces of paper with the directions on them readily available. There is no wait for the employee to find it on the Internet and print it or take a time to explain it.

- ☐ We already practice this technique
- ☐ This technique would not be suitable for our operation
- ☐ We practiced this in the past and need to jumpstart
- ☐ We should implement this technique

Assigned to: _____

Projected Date of Implementation: _____

Technique #165

Have Maps with Hotel Location Indicated on it

Tourists like to look at maps. Have a map with the hotel location already designated on it. This will save time and questions by the guests and, of course, make it easier to identify where they are. If the guests need to converse with the desk staff they can, if not, they can look at the map and figure out where to go.

☐ We already practice this technique

☐ This technique would not be suitable for our operation

☐ We practiced this in the past and need to jumpstart

☐ We should implement this technique

Assigned to: _____

Projected Date of Implementation: _____

Technique #166

Use Mobile Roulette Wheel to Reduce Perceived Waiting Times

If check-in gets busy unexpectedly, have an associate from another department roll in a mobile roulette type wheel. Have the guests waiting in line spin the wheel to determine which prize each wins. For example, prizes can range from 1–5 percent discounts on room rates.

☐   We already practice this technique

☐   This technique would not be suitable for our operation

☐   We practiced this in the past and need to jumpstart

☐   We should implement this technique

Assigned to: _____

Projected Date of Implementation: _____

1	2	3	4	5	6	7	8	9	10
11	12	13	14	15	16	17	18	19	20
21	22	23	24	25	26	27	28	29	30
31	32	33	34	35	36	37	38	39	40
41	42	43	44	45	46	47	48	49	50
51	52	53	54	55	56	57	58	59	60
61	62	63	64	65	66	67	68	69	70
71	72	73	74	75	76	77	78	79	80
81	82	83	84	85	86	87	88	89	90
91	92	93	94	95	96	97	98	99	100
101	102	103	104	105	106	107	108	109	110
111	112	113	114	115	116	117	118	119	120
121	122	123	124	125	126	127	128	129	130
131	132	133	134	135	136	137	138	139	140
141	142	143	144	145	146	147	148	149	150
151	152	153	154	155	156	157	158	159	160
161	162	163	164	165	166	**167**	**168**	**169**	**170**
171	**172**	**173**	**174**	**175**	**176**	**177**	**178**	**179**	**180**
181	**182**	**183**	**184**	**185**	**186**	**187**	**188**	**189**	

Section IV

Creating and Maintaining a Service Culture

PREVIEW

Consistently delivering high-quality service entails creating a culture within the hotel in which operating at a high level is the norm. Such a culture is fostered by reinforcing positive associate attitudes and behaviors through well-crafted incentive programs. Also, it cannot be assumed that when team members receive training on a certain service skill, they will embrace and demonstrate the skill. Rather, there are a number of means by which to maximize training transfer—the extent to which trained skills are adopted. Lastly, guests tell hotels what they want, but there is an art to gathering, understanding, and acting upon such feedback.

CHAPTER 12

Frontline Employee Incentives

*C*lassical conditioning is the term that psychologists coined nearly 100 years ago to describe how properly constructed reward systems can induce desired behaviors [24]. While a scientific foundation is appreciated, it does not require a scientist to know that hotel associates will perform at a higher level if they are properly rewarded for their efforts.

> *"You shouldn't be looking for people slipping up, you should be looking for all the good things people do and praising those."*
>
> —*Richard Branson*

Most managers who have been around the industry for any length of time would likely agree that 'carrots' work better than 'sticks' in producing a high level performance. The performance of team members is a function of this equation: PERFORMANCE = ABILITY x MOTIVATION [25]. Sections of this book address various means for managing 'ability' such as selection and training practices, but please take note of the multiplication symbol between the two terms in the above performance equation. The key reason for the multiplication symbol (as opposed to an addition symbol) is because a lack of motivation can cancel-out the effects of ability on performance. Likewise, motivation can enhance the effects of the ability.

Motivation is managed by understanding how to shape the three forms of justice as perceived by associates—distributive, procedural, and interactional justice [26]. First, distributive justice entails whether or not the associate perceives the company's resources as being allocated fairly. Second, procedural justice involves associate's perceptions regarding whether company policies are fair and uniformly applied and enforced. Lastly, interactional justice pertains to the associate's perceptions of whether supervisors and managers are rude or cooperative. Associate incentive systems are important to motivation because such systems can influence all three forms of justice perceptions.

The key to succeeding in this area lies in designing the incentive systems so that they are perceived as fair to all. Take a moment to consider the case of the front desk associate who receives a reward every time his/her name is mentioned in a positive fashion on a guest survey or on an Internet blog such as Trip Advisor (many hotels currently have such an incentive). While such a program might very well motivate a front desk agent to perform at a higher level, how will a back-of-the-house associate feel about this program? Due to a lack of guest contact, it is very unlikely that a laundry attendant or a dish room attendant will ever be mentioned on a guest survey or on the Internet. How is this incentive system fair to them? Maybe this 'incentive' program will have an opposite-than-intended demotivating effect on such back-of-the-house personnel? How can this situation be resolved? Techniques in this chapter offer potential solutions.

Technique #167

Post Positive Consumer Blog Posts for Employees to See

Employees like to be—and should be—recognized for outstanding guest service. In a section either in the staff lounge or near the time clock where the staff members tend to congregate, post all the positive comments including Trip Advisor, Social Media, Guest Survey's, letters, etc. This will recognize employees who are getting good comments and will motivate other employees to give that extra service so they too can be recognized.

☐ We already practice this technique

☐ This technique would not be suitable for our operation

☐ We practiced this in the past and need to jumpstart

☐ We should implement this technique

Assigned to: _____

Projected Date of Implementation: _____

Technique #168

Equally Reward Front and Back-of-the-House Employees

A front-of-the-house associate who is mentioned in a positive fashion on Trip Advisor should be given a reward. However, the recipient should be instructed to select a back-of-the-house associate who is worthy of receiving the equivalent reward. The front-of-the-house associate should be asked to write 2–3 sentences describing why the back-of-the-house associate is worthy of the reward. This explanation should be posted in the associate break-area (both associates are given an equivalent reward).

☐ We already practice this technique

☐ This technique would not be suitable for our operation

☐ We practiced this in the past and need to jumpstart

☐ We should implement this technique

Assigned to: _____

Projected Date of Implementation: _____

Technique #169

Establish a Uniform and Appearance Committee

The hotel should have a "uniform and appearance committee" comprised of a cross-section of managers and associates from across the hotel. The committee addresses issues regarding uniforms around the hotel. For example, should associates in a given department be permitted to wear long underwear tops on their arms in conjunction with a short sleeve uniform shirt or should long-sleeved uniform tops be issued? Knowing that fellow associates have an active voice in uniform policy provides incentive to comply.

☐ We already practice this technique

☐ This technique would not be suitable for our operation

☐ We practiced this in the past and need to jumpstart

☐ We should implement this technique

Assigned to: _____

Projected Date of Implementation: _____

Technique #170

Conduct Guest Surprise Clinics with Associates

Hold a meeting with associates in which they are shown a PowerPoint slide presentation containing photographs of the various areas of the hotel. As the associates view the photos, they should be instructed to brainstorm ideas by which guests can be surprised in the given areas (A $2 cost limit for each surprise could be the parameter used in this exercise). Associates have more incentive to carry out surprise tactics if they take part in deriving the tactics.

☐ We already practice this technique

☐ This technique would not be suitable for our operation

☐ We practiced this in the past and need to jumpstart

☐ We should implement this technique

Assigned to: _____

Projected Date of Implementation: _____

Technique #171

Have Employee Contests for Deriving Guest Surprise Ideas

Hang sketches (these are called service blueprints) of the hotel's public areas in the associate break room. Associates who can offer the most creative ideas for surprising guests by studying the sketches can win prizes.

☐ We already practice this technique

☐ This technique would not be suitable for our operation

☐ We practiced this in the past and need to jumpstart

☐ We should implement this technique

Assigned to: _____

Projected Date of Implementation: _____

Technique #172

Explain the Important Role of the Associate to His/Her Family

If an associate's family members understand how the associate's role in the hotel serves an important function in providing hospitality, then work-family conflict is reduced. Therefore, at least two times per year, management should plan a family function. During that function, management should explain to those in attendance how each associate's job is important and how it fits into the functioning of the hotel.

☐ We already practice this technique

☐ This technique would not be suitable for our operation

☐ We practiced this in the past and need to jumpstart

☐ We should implement this technique

Assigned to: _____

Projected Date of Implementation: _____

Technique #173

"I Love My Job When _____"

In an associate meeting, put the following sentence stem on a PowerPoint slide: "I love my job when _____."
Any associate who volunteers to stand in front of the group and completes the sentence wins a prize.

☐ We already practice this technique

☐ This technique would not be suitable for our operation

☐ We practiced this in the past and need to jumpstart

☐ We should implement this technique

Assigned to: _____

Projected Date of Implementation: _____

Technique #174

Implement a Housekeeping Scoring Contest

For the housekeeping department, derive a scoring system on the room inspection check sheet. The housekeeper with the highest score across a seven-day period wins either cash or a gift card to a local retail store.

☐ We already practice this technique

☐ This technique would not be suitable for our operation

☐ We practiced this in the past and need to jumpstart

☐ We should implement this technique

Assigned to: _____

Projected Date of Implementation: _____

Technique #175

Reward Departments for High Guest Satisfaction Scores

All departments should have team rewards such as pizza parties, luncheons, or gift cards when the department's target guest satisfaction survey scores are met or exceeded.

☐ We already practice this technique

☐ This technique would not be suitable for our operation

☐ We practiced this in the past and need to jumpstart

☐ We should implement this technique

Assigned to: _____

Projected Date of Implementation: _____

CHAPTER 13

Signals of Training Transfer

One study finds that 40 percent of trainees do not incorporate the training content immediately following the training; 70 percent fail to do so one year after the training; and, ultimately, only about half of training investments result in organizational improvements [27].

> *Most training programs do not have a long-run influence on employees' habits or behaviors.*

Evidently, in order for training to be effective, the content must stick. Such 'stickiness' is termed *training transfer*—the extent to which associates will apply the knowledge, skills, and behaviors communicated during the training [28]. The intent of highlighting the fact that most training is ineffective is not to dissuade firms from offering training, but rather to encourage managers to understand the drivers of training transfer.

Many of the determinants of training transfer are reinforced through techniques presented in this chapter. For example, research finds that one of the key drivers of training transfer is whether associates sense the commitment of management to the trained content [29]. Consequently, this chapter offers a number of techniques that managers can use to signal their commitment to training, excellence, and attention to detail.

Other than perceived commitment of management, other critical determinants of training transfer include items such as peer support and feedback from management. The quality of training delivery is also known to be a significant influencer regarding whether the content will stick and transform associate actions.

In summary, when training is delivered to hotel associates, there are three possible outcomes [30]. One possible outcome is an open rejection of the content by the associates—such blatant rejection is not very commonplace. A second potential outcome is termed lip-service, which describes a situation in which associates display the trained skills only when a manager is watching. Lip service is a common outcome and is very problematic because an estimated 70–80 percent of associate-guest interactions are not witnessed by management [31]. A third possible outcome of training is the associate commitment to the trained skills—this is the desired outcome. It is hoped that hotels will increase their likelihoods of achieving commitment by incorporating some/all of the techniques outlined in this chapter.

Technique #176

Maintain a Clutter-Free Office

All managers should keep their offices impeccably neat and orderly because doing so subconsciously signals the importance of cleanliness and attention to detail to associates.

☐ We already practice this technique

☐ This technique would not be suitable for our operation

☐ We practiced this in the past and need to jumpstart

☐ We should implement this technique

Assigned to: _____

Projected Date of Implementation: _____

Technique #177

Keep a Log of Guest Requests

A culture must be fostered in which it is apparent to both guests and employees that management cares about guests and their requests. All guest requests should be followed up on. A good way to do this is to create a log (example below). Not only does this log help ensure follow-up, but it gives the manager an opportunity to review requests and see if there are consistencies so these issues do not continue to occur.

Day/Date/Time/Forwarded To/Followed Up With/Follow Up With Guest/Guest Remarks

☐ We already practice this technique

☐ This technique would not be suitable for our operation

☐ We practiced this in the past and need to jumpstart

☐ We should implement this technique

Assigned to: _____

Projected Date of Implementation: _____

Technique #178

Be Visible and Converse with Guests

Most guests appreciate meeting and conversing with managers. Managers should make it a point to either assist with check-ins or roam the lobby during peak check-in or check-out. Conversations with management help personalize the check-in/check-out process. Such interactions also often uncover leads for new business and set a good example for the associates regarding the importance of interactions.

☐ We already practice this technique

☐ This technique would not be suitable for our operation

☐ We practiced this in the past and need to jumpstart

☐ We should implement this technique

Assigned to: _____

Projected Date of Implementation: _____

Technique #179

Display Attention to Detail by Cleaning the Floor

All managers should pick up lint and other small specks of debris as they move through the hotel's public areas. While very small items on the floor are likely unnoticeable to most guests, picking them up signals attention to detail to associates.

☐ We already practice this technique

☐ This technique would not be suitable for our operation

☐ We practiced this in the past and need to jumpstart

☐ We should implement this technique

Assigned to: _____

Projected Date of Implementation: _____

Technique #180

Invite a Consultant to Hold Guest Surprise Clinics with Associates

Hotel management should invite a consultant to the hotel to conduct a guest surprise clinic with associates and managers. Facilitated by the consultant, the clinic would span two hours and would involve associates and managers collectively brainstorming free/inexpensive ways to surprise guests. Management's participation in the clinic would signal their commitment to the associates. The consultant could repeat the clinic in the AM and PM to maximize associate and manager participation.

❑ We already practice this technique

❑ This technique would not be suitable for our operation

❑ We practiced this in the past and need to jumpstart

❑ We should implement this technique

Assigned to: _____

Projected Date of Implementation: _____

CHAPTER 14

Closing the Loop by Acting upon Guest Feedback

Successful hotels continually learn from the experiences of guests, associates, and managers. A decade ago, a guest would have had to have been willing to share his/her feedback with the hotel in order for management to have the opportunity to react and learn... this is no longer the case. Today, the guest-to-potential-guest word of mouth (WOM) that used to be screened from the hotel's perusal is now publicly available on Internet sites such as Trip Advisor. Consequently, in order to compete in today's hotel business, managers must actively monitor and analyze consumer-generated Internet posts in order to learn how to better serve guests. Furthermore, a number of recent studies find that responses that managers post in reply to consumer-generated content signal to potential consumers cues about the hotel's customer-centric culture [32].

Advances in technology not only allow for the text mining of guest blogs, but also the data mining of a hotel's data

> *"The ability to learn faster than your competitors may be the only sustainable competitive advantage."*
>
> —*Arie de Geus*

warehouse. Guests reveal their preferences not only through their words and writing but also through their purchase habits. Proper use of data mining software can reveal non-obvious and managerially useful patterns and trends in guest data [33]. Knowing such trends allows hotels to better serve the guest.

Of course, it is prudent to note that some of the best ways to really understand guests and their perceptions do not involve technology at all. The managers who are most in tune with guests' needs/wants, actively talk with both guests and frontline associates. There is an adage in the hotel business, which states that more can be learned through talking with 20 of a hotel's best guests for one hour each than by serving 20,000 of them. The key to the success of this approach, however, involves the level of rapport that the manager can establish with guests and associates. It is unlikely that guests or associates will share frank observations and perceptions with the manager if there is not an adequate level of rapport and comfort in the relationship.

In summary, this chapter offers a series of techniques for garnering and capitalizing on guest feedback. Some techniques are available today due to various technological advances. On the other hand, other techniques are age-old means by which to capture and understand guest feedback, but might need to be recharged at some hotel properties.

Technique #181

Understand When to Mention Your Hotel's Name When Responding to Consumer Blogs

When responding to a negative online review, the name of the hotel should never be mentioned in the response. Conversely, when responding to a positive online review, the name of the hotel should always be mentioned in the response.

☐ We already practice this technique

☐ This technique would not be suitable for our operation

☐ We practiced this in the past and need to jumpstart

☐ We should implement this technique

Assigned to: _____

Projected Date of Implementation: _____

Technique #182

Understand When to Use "I" or "We" When Responding to Consumer Blogs

When responding to a negative online review, the hotel manager should use 'I' in the online response (e.g., 'I will look into this issue'). The use of the word "I" signals ownership of the problem and resolution. On the other hand, when responding to a positive online review, the manager should use 'we' to spread the credit among the staff (e.g., 'we are very glad that you enjoyed your stay').

- ☐ We already practice this technique
- ☐ This technique would not be suitable for our operation
- ☐ We practiced this in the past and need to jumpstart
- ☐ We should implement this technique

Assigned to: _____

Projected Date of Implementation: _____

Technique #183

Paraphrase the Problem When Responding to Negative Consumer Blogs

When responding to a negative online review, the hotel manager should paraphrase the guest's concern in the online response. Such paraphrasing communicates to all those reading the response that the hotel has good listening skills.

☐ We already practice this technique

☐ This technique would not be suitable for our operation

☐ We practiced this in the past and need to jumpstart

☐ We should implement this technique

Assigned to: _____

Projected Date of Implementation: _____

Technique #184

Include a 'Relate' Statement When Responding to Negative Consumer Blogs

When responding to a negative online review, the hotel manager should attempt to include a statement detailing how s/he can relate to the problem being communicated by the guest. Including a 'relate' statement communicates to all those reading the response that the hotel is empathetic to guests' concerns.

- ☐ We already practice this technique
- ☐ This technique would not be suitable for our operation
- ☐ We practiced this in the past and need to jumpstart
- ☐ We should implement this technique

Assigned to: _____

Projected Date of Implementation: _____

Technique #185

Require One New Idea Per Week

• •

At every weekly management meeting, one manager should be required to share an innovative idea with the group that has never been attempted in the hotel.

☐   We already practice this technique

☐   This technique would not be suitable for our operation

☐   We practiced this in the past and need to jumpstart

☐   We should implement this technique

Assigned to: _____

Projected Date of Implementation: _____

Technique #186

Graph Guest Problems According to Frequency and Seriousness

Guest problems should be tracked and plotted on a graph according to their frequency and seriousness. A cross-departmental team of 6–8 line-level associates and managers should be created to derive strategies for fixing the most pressing problems based upon frequency and/or seriousness.

☐ We already practice this technique

☐ This technique would not be suitable for our operation

☐ We practiced this in the past and need to jumpstart

☐ We should implement this technique

Assigned to: _____

Projected Date of Implementation: _____

Technique #187

Text Mine Consumer Blogs for Trends

Hotel management should contract with a 3rd party vendor (e.g., Revinate) so that consumers' blog postings can be analyzed for trends. Many of these 3rd party vendor products also enable management to monitor trends in competitors' blog postings.

☐ We already practice this technique

☐ This technique would not be suitable for our operation

☐ We practiced this in the past and need to jumpstart

☐ We should implement this technique

Assigned to: _____

Projected Date of Implementation: _____

Technique #188

Data Mine the Centralized Reservations System for Trends

Hotel management should data mine its centralized reservation system to identify non-obvious patterns and trends in guests' habits and preferences. The results of such data mining can be used to better serve guests, but also to build an enhanced understanding of proper timing and placement of marketing messages. Chain affiliated hotels likely already have data mining services available to them. Managers at independent hotels can be taught some basic data mining functions by a consultant. The extent of data mining capabilities offered by 3rd party management companies appears to vary widely across the industry.

☐ We already practice this technique

☐ This technique would not be suitable for our operation

☐ We practiced this in the past and need to jumpstart

☐ We should implement this technique

Assigned to: _____

Projected Date of Implementation: _____

Technique #189

Utilize the Front Desk as a Listening Post

Front desk associates should consider their work area a "listening post" from which they can overhear conversations between guests. Many guests may be reluctant to actively voice complaints to hotel staff, but discuss various issues among themselves (e.g., the ice machine was too noisy; the sidewalks leading to the parking lot were too icy). Such information should be entered into the logbook and denoted as "listening post feedback."

☐ We already practice this technique

☐ This technique would not be suitable for our operation

☐ We practiced this in the past and need to jumpstart

☐ We should implement this technique

Assigned to: _____

Projected Date of Implementation: _____

Concluding Remarks

• • • • • • • • • • • • • • • •

Why 189 techniques? 180 degrees signifies a turn-around. Whether you are at a troubled property that is in need of a customer service culture turn-around, or at a property that performs well and only needs continuous fine-tuning, we hope that you found a portion of the techniques in this book applicable to your property. The extra nine techniques are included because some do not relate to all hotels—for example, your property may not have a swimming pool (techniques #109 and #110).

Because many of the techniques described in this book derive from properties from various points around the world, many of the techniques would delightfully surprise guests if applied at your property. The surprise is a powerful emotion; when guests are surprised, they pay full attention to the transaction. Consider the study that connected subjects to MRI machines and then squirted a pattern of drinks into their mouths: water-juice-water-juice-water-juice… When the pattern was broken with water-water or juice-juice, the MRI machines lit up like Christmas trees due to the brain activity caused by the surprise [34]. The moral is that when people are surprised, they pay full attention.

Evidently, surprise tactics are not useful if frontline associates do not have the ability and motivation to routinely use them in interactions with guests. For this reason, techniques related to areas of employee recruitment, selection, training, and evaluation are also key components in this book. As we all know, exceptional customer service is a team effort. But... the managers are the leaders... all managers are leaders (leading in a positive or negative direction). The managers set the tone—the foundation for the service culture. Stating that a manager is not a leader would be analogous to a street sign that reads, "sign not in use." Any sign that someone can see is "in use," similarly, all managers are leaders because they set the tone that anchors the culture.

Hopefully, the techniques in this book will reinforce the anchor. Good Luck!

References

1. Gladwell, M. (2008). *Outliers*. Backbay Books: New York.

2. Kaufman, R. (2012). *Uplifting Service*. New York: Evolve Publishing.

3. Corporate Dilemma. The quotation in this call-out box is from a cartoon available on the Internet titled 'Corporate Dilemma: Investing in Employees.' The signature of the author of the cartoon in not legible in the cartoon.

4. Saks, A. M., & Belcourt, M. (2006). An investigation of training activities and transfer of training in organizations. *Human Resource Management*, *45*(4), 629–648.

5. Crotts, J. C., & Magnini, V. P. (2011). The customer delight construct: is surprise essential?. *Annals of Tourism Research*, *38*(2), 719–722.

6. Johnson, S., & Blanchard, K. (1986). *The One-Minute Manager*. Video Publishing House.

7. *The One Minute Manager* at KennethBlanchard.com.

8. Gladwell, M. (2007). *Blink: The Power of Thinking Without Thinking*. Hachette Digital, Inc.

9. Nisbett, R. E., & Wilson, T. D. (1977). The halo effect: Evidence for unconscious alteration of judgments. *Journal of Personality and Social Psychology*, *35*(4), 250.

10. Rabin, M., & Schrag, J. L. (1999). First impressions matter: A model of confirmatory bias. *Quarterly Journal of Economics*, 37–82.

11. Kano, N., Seraku, N., Takahashi, F., & Tsuji, S. (1984). Attractive quality and must-be quality. *Journal of the Japanese Society for Quality Control, 14*(2), 147–156.

12. Oliver, R. (1980). "A Cognitive Model of the Antecedents and Consequences of Satisfaction Decisions." *Journal of Marketing Research, 17*, 460–469.

13. West, J. J., Olsen, M. D., & Tse, E. C. Y. (2008). *Strategic Management in the Hospitality Industry*. Prentice Hall.

14. Magnini, Vincent P. (2014). Surprise! The Secret to Customer Loyalty in the Service Sector. Business Expert Press: New York, NY.

15. Magnini, Vincent P., & Candice E. (2012). Delivering an Experience through Service Excellence: A Training Manual for Hotel Associates. ISBN: 978-0-615-58267-2.

16. McCollough, M. A., & Bharadwaj, S. G. (1992). The recovery paradox: an examination of consumer satisfaction in relation to disconfirmation, service quality, and attribution based theories. *Marketing Theory and Applications, 3*, 119.

17. Magnini, V. P., Ford, J. B., Markowski, E. P., & Honeycutt Jr., E. D. (2007). The service recovery paradox: justifiable theory or smoldering myth?. *Journal of Services Marketing, 21*(3), 213–225.

18. Magnini, Ford, Markowski, and Honeycutt, op. cit.

19. Magnini, Ford, Markowski, and Honeycutt, op. cit.

20. Magnini, Ford, Markowski, and Honeycutt, op. cit.

21. Bitner, M. J., Booms, B. H., & Tetreault, M. S. (1990). The service encounter: diagnosing favorable and unfavorable incidents. *The Journal of Marketing*, 71–84.

22. Edinger, S. (2013). Four principles for great sales forecasts. Forbes (6/3/2013).

23. Zackay, D., & Hornik, J. (1991). "How much time did you wait in line? A time perception perspective," in J.C. Chebat and V. Venkatesan (eds.), *Time and Consumer Behavior*. Montreal: University of Quebec at Montreal.

24. Pavlov, I. P. (1927/1960). *Conditional Reflexes*. New York: Dover Publications (the 1960 edition is not an unaltered republication of the 1927 translation by Oxford University Press http://psychclassics.yorku.ca/Pavlov/).

25. Magnini, V. (2013). Performance Enhancers: Twenty Essential Habits for Service Businesses. Tate Publishing: Mustang Oklahoma.

26. Blodgett, J. G., Hill, D. J., & Tax, S. S. (1997). The effects of distributive, procedural, and interactional justice on postcomplaint behavior. *Journal of Retailing*, *73*(2), 185–210.

27. Burke, L., & Hutchins, H. (2007). "Training transfer: An integrative literature review." *Human Resource Development Review*, *6*(3), 263–296.

28. Saks, A. M., & Belcourt, M. (2006). "An investigation of training activities and transfer of training in organizations." *Human Resource Management*, *45*, 629–648.

29. Burke, L., & Hutchins, H., op. cit.

30. Magnini, V. (2013), op. cit.

31. Deshpande, R., & Raina, A. (2011). "The ordinary heroes of the Taj." *Harvard Business Review*, December 1, 2011.

32. Min, H., Lim, Y., & Magnini, V. P. (2014). Factors Affecting Customer Satisfaction in Responses to Negative Online Hotel Reviews The Impact of Empathy, Paraphrasing, and Speed. *Cornell Hospitality Quarterly*, 1938965514560014.

33. Magnini, V. P., Honeycutt, E. D., & Hodge, S. K. (2003). Data mining for hotel firms: Use and limitations. *The Cornell Hotel and Restaurant Administration Quarterly*, *44*(2), 94–105.

34. Berns, G. S., McClure, S. M., Pagnoni, G., & Montague, P. R. (2001). Predictability modulates human brain response to reward. *The Journal of Neuroscience*, *21*(8), 2793–2798.